DEVELOPING
FLUENCY
IN ENGLISH

DEVELOPING FLUENCY IN ENGLISH

With Sentence-Combining Practice in Nominalization

Ruth Crymes

*Department of English as a
Second Language
University of Hawaii*

Gary James

*English Department
Kyoto YMCA Gakuin*

Larry Smith

*Culture Learning Institute
East-West Center*

Harvey Taylor

*Department of East Asian Languages
University of Hawaii*

Prentice-Hall, Inc., *Englewood Cliffs, New Jersey*

Library of Congress Cataloging in Publication Data
Main entry under title:

Developing fluency in English.

    1. English language—Text-books for foreigners.
I. Crymes, Ruth H.
PE1128.D44   428'.2'4   73–17362
ISBN 0–13–204826–4

PE 1128
D44

10   9   8   7   6   5   4   3

Prentice-Hall International, Inc., *London*
Prentice-Hall of Australia, Pty, Ltd., *Sydney*
Prentice-Hall of Canada, Ltd., *Toronto*
Prentice-Hall of India Private Limited, *New Delhi*
Prentice-Hall of Japan, Inc., *Tokyo*

Acknowledgments

For all the help that they received in the development of this book the authors wish to say *mahalo nui loa* (a big thank you)

to the students in the Fall 1968 ESL Materials Development class at the University of Hawaii who helped the authors clarify their ideas of the significance of the competence/performance distinction in teaching and learning a second language;

to Jason Alter and Ted Plaister of the Department of English as a Second Language at the University of Hawaii for making experimental classes available and for their support and encouragement;

to Sylvia Cowan, Lee Cramer, Richard Day, and Carole Goss Urzua for their patience and perceptions in teaching early drafts of the materials;

to John F. O'Donnell, who, while a student at Temple University, gave us thorough and helpful criticism of an early draft;

to Jason Alter, Roy Collier, Donna Gobert, Joan Petraglia Poepoe, and James Wilson for their cooperation and assistance in the testing and evaluation of the materials;

to the University of Hawaii for a Curriculum Development Grant which helped in the testing and evaluation of the materials;

to Frances Ascencio, Kathleen Fukao, Craig Koizumi, Carolyn Mott Kurisu, Ivan Propst, Arthur Recchi, David Rickard, and Charles Whitley for their generous help in recording the tapes;

to the students in the English Language Institute at the University of Hawaii and to the Asian and Pacific administrators and teacher educators at the Culture Learning Institute of the East-West Center who were the most knowledgeable critics of our early drafts;

to the editorial staff of Prentice-Hall, Inc., for friendly support and guidance throughout;

and to Naomi Hirata, Marilyn Mitobe, and Karen Shiroma for skillful assistance in preparing the manuscript.

R.C.
G.J.
L.S.
H.T.

To the Teacher

This book is designed to help high intermediate and advanced students of English as a second language improve their fluency in English through two avenues: (1) practice in listening and speaking in informal situations, where emphasis is on *what* is said, and (2) exercises incorporating systematic presentation of one aspect of English sentence embedding, that is, nominalization—exercises which are intended to help the students internalize some of the system of English syntax.

Thus, the first avenue is practice in performance, in actually using English. The second avenue is development of competence in English nominalizing processes. And although the performance emphasized in this book is speaking and listening, competence in nominalization underlies reading and writing as well. So the knowledge that the student gains, both intuitively and explicitly, about the nominalizing process in English through doing these exercises should provide him with a resource for developing fluency in either the oral or written mode. By *fluency* is meant the ability to understand and produce sentences—either spoken or written—which contain embedded sentences; it is the ability to compress a number of ideas into a single sentence and to understand sentences which contain ideas so compressed.

The main features of this book are as follows:

1. The text is divided into two parts: Part I "Performing in English," and Part II "Sentence Study: Developing Competence."
2. Practice in *using* the language is kept separate from *study about* the language, on the assumption that the relationship between the two is indirect. Experimental evidence supporting this assumption can be found in John C. Mellon, *Transformational Sentence Combining, A Method of Enhancing the Development of Syntactic Fluency*, Final Report, Cooperative Research Project No. 5–8418, Office of English Education and Laboratory for Research in Instruction, Graduate School of Education, Harvard University, Cambridge, Massachusetts, 1967. This study was published by the National Council of Teachers of English at Champaign, Illinois, in 1968. The subjects of Mellon's study were native-speaking seventh-graders, not second-language learners, and they were children whose native

language was still in the process of development, not people who already had mature knowledge of their own language. However, field-testing of *Developing Fluency in English* has indicated that with adult second-language learners, study about the nominalizing processes in English does in fact correlate with an increased comprehension and use of nominalizations.

3. Each of the nine lessons of Part I is built around a set of texts on a topic chosen because it stimulates talk among the students. The nine topics are Proverbs, Folk Medicine, Nonverbal Communication, Intelligence, Propaganda, Words in Context, Forms of Address, The Environment and the Automobile, and Food for Thought (i.e., food fads).

4. Each lesson has a set of four texts:
   (1) Reading text—either an original or an adaptation
   (2) Listening text—the information in the reading text presented in oral style
   (3) Summary—brief presentation of the main ideas of the listening text to be used as a preview at the start of each lesson to provide a mental "set"
   (4) Discussion text—an unrehearsed, unedited discussion by native speakers related to the topic of the lesson.
   Texts (2), (3), and (4) are on tape, and a transcription of each tape is provided in the lessons. There is no grammatical structuring of the language of these texts, though the language of the listening texts is in general structurally simpler than that of the reading texts. The aim is for the students to use the ideas in the texts as a take-off for speaking activities, not to understand in detail everything that is in them.

5. Each lesson provides suggestions for several speaking activities that will engage the students in real communication with each other, on the assumption that students learn a second language more effectively through their attempts at real communication than through drills which simulate communication.

6. Each lesson has vocabulary exercises built around words ocurring in the texts, showing their meanings in the texts and also in other contexts.

7. The purpose of the sentence study exercises (Part II) is to give students insight into ways that sentences are embedded in other sentences, especially through nominalization transforms. The grammatical material in these exercises is based on the analysis of nominals by Zeno Vendler in *Adjectives and Nominalizations* (Papers on Formal Linguistics, No. 5, The Hague, Mouton, 1968) and by Paul Kiparsky and Carol Kiparsky in "Fact," in *Semantics: An Interdisciplinary Reader*, Danny Steinberg and Leon Jakobovits, eds. (Cambridge and New York, Cambridge University Press, 1971). There are, however, many theoretical problems in the analysis of

nominals, and so these sources have been used in a pragmatic way and certain adaptations have been made to meet pedagogical needs.

8. The vocabulary and sentence study exercises are designed for self-study and self-checking and have built-in allowances for students of varying abilities.

9. The vocabulary and sentence study exercises are designed to encourage the student to think about the *meanings* of the sentences as he works with them.

10. The lessons can be taken up in any order. No lesson is dependent on any other lesson.

11. The teaching time for each lesson is about 5 hours, but the materials provided are ample for up to 10 hours of work, depending upon both the number of speaking activities used and the amount of class time spent in discussing the homework. In the beginning, the average student will probably need to spend two hours on the homework for each lesson. Later on students will be able to do the work faster.

Each of the nine lessons in Part I has six parts: Preview, Reading Text, Listening Text, Discussion Text, Speaking Activities, and Vocabulary Study. The Sentence Study (Part II of the text) may be studied along with the lessons after each lesson is completed. Answers to the Vocabulary Study and Sentence Study are provided for the student following each set of exercises.

Each of these parts is described below, with suggested procedures for teaching:

Preview

What it is. The preview consists of (1) a listing of key vocabulary items, (2) a transcription of the taped summary, and (3) questions on the taped summary of the listening text.

Aim. The aim is to provide the student with a mental "set," that is, an expectation about what he is going to learn in the listening (and reading) texts, to help him in comprehending them. The assumption is that if the student has some idea of what the content of the text is going to be he can make educated guesses about what the texts say even when he does not pick up all the language signals. Even a native speaker can have trouble comprehending parts of what he hears or reads unless he has some general idea of what it is all about. In fact, experiments have shown that people sometimes hear what they are told they will hear, even though what they in fact listen to says something quite different from what they have been told to expect. It does not seem reasonable to demand of nonnative speakers what one does not demand of native speakers; hence the provision for establishing "set" through the discussion of key vocabulary items and the taped (or read) summary.

Suggested procedures.   First discuss the vocabulary items listed at the beginning of the preview. Talk about the meanings of these items within the context of the lesson. Then go over the questions that the student will be asked to answer after he has listened to or read the summary. Finally present the summary. This can be done in different ways: play the taped summary either before or after the students have seen the summary in print or have the students read the summary either silently or orally. The length of time spent on going over the questions will depend on the teacher's assessment of how much background information the students need before proceeding to the listening text.

Reading Text

What it is.   The reading text is sometimes an excerpt from a longer work, sometimes a complete article, and in one case a summary of a longer work. Footnotes indicate the source of each reading text. The reading texts were chosen primarily on the basis of their content—they are the source of the content of all the activities and exercises. They vary in reading difficulty.

Aim.   A reading text is included in each lesson to make the original source of the listening text available to teachers and students for optional reading. The texts also provide examples of unsimplified English and a source for contrasting written and spoken English, since the listening text is an oral version of the reading text.

Suggested procedures.   Reading the reading text is not essential to any lesson. The teacher, at his discretion, might assign some of the texts for homework. It is recommended that if a reading text is assigned as homework, no class time be taken for discussion of it. The students should read it on their own for the gist of what it says—for whatever they can get out of it—without worrying about details. Some of the vocabulary study exercises make use of parts of the reading texts, but the student, in these exercises, has only to work with the words and expressions in the context of individual sentences. So, in these exercises, he will be dealing with only parts of the reading text.

Listening Text

What it is.   The listening text is a restatement of the main ideas of the reading text by a native speaker. The native speaker has, in each case, thought in advance about what he is going to say. Hence, the language is premeditated rather than spontaneous. However, the vocabulary and sentence structure are characteristic of spoken, rather than written English. The language is something like the language of a lecture or talk which has been thought out in advance and then presented orally with or without notes.

Aim. The purpose of the listening text is to provide listening comprehension practice on a topic that the students have had some acquaintance with (through the preview) and to provide subject matter for the speaking activities and for the sentences in the sentence study exercises.

Suggested procedures. The listening text may be presented and discussed in class with or without the accompanying tape (see suggested procedures on page 2). The teacher can have the students listen to the text as many times as seems helpful. After the initial presentatin and discussion, the teacher may want to play the tape or present the text himself orally on subsequent days, to provide additional listening practice.

Discussion Text

What it is. The discussion text is an unrehearsed, unpremeditated conversation between native speakers on some aspect of the subject matter of the listening text. It is taped, and a transcription is provided in each lesson.

Aim. One aim is to provide practice in listening to spontaneous native-speaker English. Spontaneous speech contains hesitations, false starts, interruptions of one speaker by another, and grammatical tangles. Yet, native speakers understand each other's language (though, of course, they may not always understand each other's ideas). Another aim is to provide practice in obtaining nonlinguistic information about people from the way they talk to each other, that is, information about such things as the age and education, the relationship, and the personalities of the speakers.

Suggested procedures. Go over any study helps that are given in the notes preceding the text in each lesson. Also go over the questions about the speakers that the students will be asked to respond to on the basis of cues in the conversation. Then play the tape several times, allowing the students to follow the transcription with their eyes, if this helps them to understand. Then discuss the questions, and, if the students are interested, have them continue the discussion that they have just heard on tape.

Speaking Activities

What they are. In each lesson there are from four to six speaking activities listed. These are open-ended discussion questions on topics related to the topic of the listening text. The students can discuss most of the questions on the basis of their own experience.

Aim.   The aim is to give the students an opportunity to communicate with each other in realistic communication situations with primary attention to *what* is said rather than *how* it is said.

Suggested procedures.   It is recommended that normally three or four class periods be spent on the speaking activities of each lesson. Teachers and students should not feel under any compulsion to do all the speaking activities. Rather, they should pursue the ones that they are most interested in. It may be that, in some cases, if the subject of a lesson is of particular interest, the class might want to spend extra days talking about it. The teacher might want to show a movie related to the subject or bring in related reading materials. The handling of the speaking activities should be flexible, the main guideline being that the students should carry the burden of the talk, with the teacher in the role of resource person and moderator. Various types of class organization can be used: pairs of students working together and then making presentations to the whole class; small group discussions going on simultaneously; panel discussions; debates. The teacher can exercise his ingenuity in creating situations which require students to speak to and understand each other. The teacher can stand ready to "put words in a student's mouth" when the opportunity arises to do so. In this way, the student will hear a model of English at the time he feels a need for it. But under no circumstances should discussion of grammar and pronunciation interfere with the communication going on. The students should concern themselves with what they want to say, and not be inhibited by concern for correctness in how they are saying it. If a class is working on writing as well as speaking, some of the speaking activities can be used as writing activities, again with the emphasis on what is said—on communicating ideas.

Nine topics are presented in this text, but the number of possible topics is unlimited. Timely articles on pollution, drug abuse, population, and so forth, could easily be discussed using the same format.

Vocabulary Exercises

What they are.   Each lesson has some vocabulary exercises over items which occur in the listening and/or reading texts.

Aim.   These exercises give the student further exposure to words and expressions found in the listening and reading texts. They give practice in using those items both in the meaning they have in the texts and in the meanings they may have in other contexts. A special effort has been made to deal with the form and distribution of the vocabulary items as well as with their lexical meanings.

Suggested procedures. It is recommended that the students do these exercises on their own as homework. Answers are provided for self-checking. Each time a new lesson is begun, the teacher can assign the students to start working on the vocabulary (and sentence study) exercises and can set a completion date.

Sentence Study (Part II)

What they are. These exercises give practice in nominalization; that is, they give practice in taking one sentence, changing it into a clause or into a gerund or infinitive phrase, and inserting it into another sentence. The subject matter of the sentences is related to the topic of the lesson (this is the only connection between the sentence study exercises and the reading and listening texts), and each sentence has an exercise which checks the ability of the student to comprehend the meaning of sentences of the type studied.

Aim. The aim is to help the student develop competence in the nominalizing processes of English. It is expected that by doing these exercises, the student's competence will develop to the point that he will be better able to comprehend and produce English sentences which contain nominalizations. No attempt is made to relate the work in the sentence study exercises with the communication that goes on in connection with the speaking activities, since language is stimulus-free, and it is therefore not possible to force production of particular types of sentences in a real communication situation. Any effect that the sentence study exercises may have on the student's performance will be indirect.

Suggested procedures. The student should do these exercises and check them on his own outside class—the answers are provided for him following each set of exercises. As with the vocabulary exercises, it is suggested that the teacher, when he begins each new lesson, assign the sentence study exercises to be done as homework, to be completed by the time the lesson as a whole is completed. It is recommended that at the completion of each lesson, the teacher devote some class time to going over any questions that the students may have about any of the sentence study exercises. It is also recommended that at the completion of each lesson the teacher give a quiz over the sentence study exercises, consisting of (1) dictation of some of the sentences from the exercises, with the teacher dictating each sentence only once, and (2) portions (or wholes) of the Summary Exercise and the What about Meaning Exercise simply copied out and duplicated for the students to do without reference to their books.

The aim of *Developing Fluency in English* is to give the nonnative English speaker practice in expressing his ideas in English in informal communication situations. The teacher should feel free to organize the material, supplement it or replace it in any way that will best accomplish that aim.

Contents

To the Teacher

Turning sentences into subjects and objects: *that, ing,* and
for-to
   I. Turning sentences into subjects by using *that, ing,* and
   for-to

passives. Changing passives into sentences beginning with *it*

IV. Changing sentences with *that*-expression subjects into sentences beginning with *it*

V. Summary

VI. What about meaning?

Turning sentences into objects: *ing*-expressions and plain verbs

I. Turning sentences into objects by using either *ing* or a plain verb or by changing the verb into a noun, after the verbs *see, hear, feel, watch*

II. Comparing completed actions signalled by the plain verb

III. Using plain verbs after *make* and *let*

IV. Using *ing-expressions* after *by, in,* and *at*

V. Summary

VI. What about meaning?

Turning sentences into subjects and complements: *(for) to* expressions with adjectives and nouns, and variations thereof

I. Turning sentences into complements of adjectives; other ways of saying the same thing. Adjectives: *good(of), stupid(of), thoughtful(of),* etc.; *good(for), hard(for), difficult(for),* etc.

II. *It is possible (for-to)* compared with *it is possible (that)*

III. Turning sentences into complements of nouns; other ways of saying the same thing

Turning sentences into objects and complements: *that/ing, that/to,* and split sentences

I. Turning sentences into objects by using *that* and *ing* and the split sentence paraphrase—after *forget, remember, remind (someone) about*

II. Turning sentences into complements by using *that* and *to* and the split sentence paraphrase—after *forget, remember, remind (someone) about*

III. Using *that, ing,* and *to* expressions

IV. Summary

V. What about meaning?

DEVELOPING FLUENCY IN ENGLISH

Part I

PERFORMING IN ENGLISH

I am not a good mimic and I have worked now in many different cultures. I am a very poor speaker of any language, but I always know whose pig is dead, and, when I work in a native society, I know what people are talking about and I treat it seriously and I respect them, and this in itself establishes a great deal more rapport, very often, than the correct accent. I have worked with other field workers who were far, far better linguists than I, and the natives kept on saying they couldn't speak the language, although they said I could! Now, if you had a recording it would be proof positive I couldn't, but nobody knew it! You see, we don't need to teach people to speak like natives, you need to make the other people believe they can, so they can talk to them, and then they learn.

Margaret Mead, from the Discussion Session on Language
Teaching in *Approaches to Semiotics*, ed.
by Thomas A. Sebeok, Alfred S. Hayes, and
Mary Catherine Bateson (The Hague: Mouton
& Co., 1964), p. 189.

Organization of the Lessons and Directions

Each of the nine lessons in Part I has five parts: (1) Preview; (2) Reading Text; (2) Listening Text; (3) Discussion; (4) Speaking Activities; and (5) Vocabulary Study. For each lesson there is a tape recording of a summary of the Listening Text (a transcript of the recording is provided in the Preview), the Listening Text itself, and the Discussion.

First, do the *Preview*, following the directions provided. The purpose of the Preview is to introduce you to the main ideas of the Reading and Listening Texts. Doing the Preview will give you a "mental set" which will help you "tune in" to the ideas of the Reading and Listening Texts.

After you do the Preview, your teacher will ask you to do one or more of the following activities one or more times.

1. Read the *Reading Text*.
2. Listen to the *Listening Text* while looking at it.
3. Listen to the *Listening Text* without looking at it.

The purpose of these activities is to give you practice in reading and listening and to give you information about the topic of the lesson.

Next, listen to the *Discussion* and answer the questions which accompany it. The Discussion in each lesson is carried out by native speakers and is recorded and transcribed exactly as it was spoken. Each Discussion is an example of "real" use of language, with false starts, hesitations, and mixed-up syntax.

Then, turn to the *Speaking Activities*. These are suggestions for things to talk about. You don't need to do all of the Speaking Activities. Select the ones that interest you most. Try to talk and get across your ideas without worrying too much about the correctness of your grammar. And don't worry if the talk strays to other topics. The aim here is for you to communicate your ideas to others and to understand the ideas that they are communicating to you.

Finally, do the *Vocabulary Study*. You can do it by yourself or in a small group. The answers are provided, and so you can correct your work yourself.

When you finish a lesson in Part I, turn to the corresponding Sentence Study Lesson in Part II and do it.

The lessons in Part I may be taken up in any order.

Proverbs

Discuss these key terms:

proverb
comment
maxim

Listen to or read the summary below. Then try to answer the questions that follow.

SUMMARY

Proverbs are wise sayings. They comment about life in general—but only in a few words. Some people believe that human beings everywhere have certain things in common. As a result, proverbs meaning basically the same thing are found in many languages of the world. No one knows why some languages have many proverbs while others have few.

QUESTIONS

1. What do proverbs comment about?
2. How (in what way) are the ideas in proverbs expressed?
3. Why are proverbs which mean essentially the same thing found in many languages of the world?
4. Why are many proverbs found in some languages and very few in others?

For suggested directions for doing these lessons see page 2 of this book.

Reading Text—Proverbs*

(1) "Too many cooks spoil the broth"—so goes a proverb that is as familiar to most Americans as its meaning. The Iranians expressed the same thought with different words: "Two midwives will deliver a baby with a crooked head." So do the Italians: "With so many roosters crowing, the sun never comes up." The Russians: "With seven nurses, the child goes blind." And the Japanese: "Too many boatmen run the boat up to the top of the mountain."

(2) These lean, didactic, aphoristic statements, so varied in their language, seem to distill a universal wisdom. In the Samoan fishing culture, which is dependent on the canoe, islanders would have no difficulty in recognizing the kinship of the English proverb, "It never rains but it pours," to one of their own: "It leaks at the gunwale, it leaks in the keel." From the Biblical injunction, "An eye for an eye, a tooth for a tooth," it is only a short and negotiable step to an old saying of the Nandi tribe in East Africa: "A goat's hide buys a goat's hide and a gourd a gourd."

(3) Can it be that the proverb, literally "before the word"—provides a clue to the common denominator of all human thought? This possibility has been raised by George B. Milner, 50, a linguist at the University of London's School of Oriental and African Studies.

(4) . . . Milner's interest in the proverb began in 1955, when he flew to the South Pacific to compile the first Samoan dictionary since 1862. There he found a rigidly stratified culture that relied on the proverb as a guide through the thicket of social life. The Samoans had proverbs for every human exchange, says Milner: "To pay respect, to express pleasure, sympathy, regret, to make people laugh, to blame or criticize, to apologize, to insult, thank, cajole, ask a favor, say farewell." Intrigued, he collected thousands of these pithy sayings.

(5) Back in England, Milner compared his Samoan stock with the proverbs current in Europe, and was struck by the many similarities in structure, rhythm and content. It was almost as if the proverb shared a common source. Since this was culturally impossible, Milner considered another potential origin: The universality of human thought.

(6) Regardless of their genesis, Milner argues, the best proverbs easily transcend ethnic and geographic barriers. They deal in the fundamental stuff of life: love and war, birth and death, sickness and health, work and play. . . .

(7) . . . It remains a mystery, moreover, why some civilizations are rich in proverbs and others are not. Why did the Incas, the Mayans and nearly all the Indian tribes of North America produce such a meager crop of

*"Language: The Wild Flowers of Thought," reprinted by permission from TIME, The Weekly Newsmagazine; Copyright Time Inc. 1969.

proverbs, when the Spaniards, the Samoans, the Arabs and the Chinese were minting them by the thousands?*

Listening Text—Proverbs

(1) Almost every language has its share of proverbs or wise sayings. Listen to this popular English proverb: "Too many cooks spoil the broth." Compare it to how people living in Iran say the same thing: "Two midwives will deliver a baby with a crooked head." Italians say: "With so many roosters crowing, the sun never comes up." Russians say: "With seven nurses the child goes blind." And finally the Japanese say: "Too many boatmen run the boat up to the top of the mountain."

(2) These statements say a great deal in a very few words. But the surprising thing is that basically all the preceding wise sayings were very similar in meaning. Is it possible that all human beings (no matter what language they speak) share certain feelings about life in common and thus produce like-sounding proverbs? Some people think so.

(3) They say that the best proverbs—no matter what the language—have certain characteristics in common: they all are concerned about life in general and cover the vast range of human endeavor—love and war, birth and death, sickness and health, and work and play.

(4) No one knows why some people have few proverbs (like many of the Indian tribes of North America) while others have thousands (such as Spaniards, Samoans, Arabs, and Chinese).

(5) Have you ever compared English proverbs with wise sayings in your language?

Discussion—Proverbs

NOTES AND QUESTIONS ON DISCUSSION TAPE AND TEXT

This is a conversation between two good friends, both from the Midwest, about the uses of proverbs in American English.

Some questions to explore:

Is this a scholarly discussion or an informal chat?
How well educated are the speakers?
What age do you think the speakers are?

Study helps:

"as extended or extensive" means "as widespread"
"too trite" means "used too much"
"highly eroded" means "destroyed to a large extent"
"wiped out" means "destroyed"
Notice that toward the end of the discussion, the word "Mayan" is mispronounced.

DISCUSSION

GARY: Ivan, have you ever wondered why some cultures have more proverbs than others? Say for example, the Mayans and the Incas and the North American Indian tribes seem to have fewer proverbs than cultures like the, well, the Arabians, like the Chinese. I wonder why this is.

IVAN: What would you say about our . . . our own culture? Would you say we're a culture that's rich in proverbs or one that lacks proverbs?

GARY: I think we, we have a rich heritage of proverbs—the Benjamin Franklin maxims, proverbs, wise sayings have been handed down to us.

IVAN: Well, I think the fact that we're no longer creating proverbs today maybe says something . . . maybe perhaps explains to some extent why proverbs in certain cultures were not as extended or extensive as in other cultures.

GARY: Mm, hmm. Mm, hmm. That's true. I wonder why we are not creating as many proverbs as, say, we did in the seventeen and eighteen hundreds. I agree with you. I don't think there're nearly as many. I can't think of any. I'm sure there are some, but I wonder why this is so.

IVAN: Yeah. Well, I think we all know a great many proverbs. If we sit down, we can think of some that we can . . . we can list. But we don't seem to . . . to use them to explain things. We find many times that they're far too trite and too simple—too general. Today we're much more sophisticated, you might say, and analytical, and therefore we don't use proverbs to explain things the way, say, our grandfathers and parents did.

GARY: Life is too complicated now to just quote a . . . a simple proverb to take care of things.

IVAN: Right, and maybe to some extent that's why the North American Indians and the Mayans among others don't have as many proverbs. At least there's no record of as many proverbs. Since their own culture . . . their traditions were highly eroded and they . . . they were wiped out during this era of change.

GARY: Mm, hmm. Well, that's interesting.

Speaking Activities—Proverbs

I

Answer on the basis of the Listening Text:

What does the English proverb "Too many cooks spoil the broth" advise people to do?

What are some of the characteristics of proverbs that the author mentions?

What may the similarity between proverbs in various languages indicate?

What struck you as interesting in the Listening Text?

Here is a reference list of some English proverbs that you may want to refer to when you are doing the speaking activities below:

1. Too many cooks spoil the broth.
2. Birds of a feather flock together.
3. When in Rome, do as the Romans do.
4. A stitch in time saves nine.
5. A rolling stone gathers no moss.
6. Don't count your chickens before they're hatched.
7. Silence is golden.
8. His bark is worse than his bite.
9. Haste makes waste.
10. A bird in the hand is worth two in the bush.
11. Make hay while the sun shines.
12. Don't cry over spilt milk.

II

Think of a proverb in your language. Translate it into English and see if your classmates can understand its meaning. If they are not successful in guessing its meaning, explain it to them.

III

Can you think of some proverbs in your language that are similar in meaning to some proverbs in English? Do they express the meanings in the same way? Discuss.

IV

Working with a partner, select an English proverb, explain its meaning in your own words, and compose a short dialog using the proverb in order to show a situation where it might be used.

For example, "Too many cooks spoil the broth" means that "having more than one person direct an activity often causes the activity to end in failure" or that "one boss is better than many bosses."

This proverb could be used in a situation like the following:

JOE: I'll be responsible for cleaning the house.

MAY: So will I.

JOE: O.K. But remember that too many cooks can spoil the broth.

V

Do you have any idea why some cultures are rich in proverbs while others are not? Would you call your native culture rich in proverbs? Discuss.

VI

How are proverbs passed on from one generation to the next? How and when did you learn the proverbs that you know?

Vocabulary Study—Proverbs

NOTE: L-2 = Listening Text, paragraph 2; R-3 = Reading Text, paragraph 3, and so forth. Words and sentences marked in this way can be found in the text and paragraph so indicated.

   I. *didactic, aphoristic, and lean* (R-2)

      1. Which of the following statements is didactic? Place a check in front of it.

         _____ a. Early to bed and early to rise
                Makes a man healthy, wealthy, and wise.

_____ b. I always get up early.

2. Which of the following statements is aphoristic? Place a check in front of it.

_____ a. If you hurry too much, you may do something that will need to be redone, and you may therefore require more time than if you had gone more slowly in the first place.

_____ b. Haste makes waste.

3. Which of the following statements is lean? Place a check in front of it.

_____ a. One aspect of the book which he found very puzzling was its last chapter.

_____ b. The last chapter of the book puzzled him.

II. *share* (noun)
Fill in the blank in each sentence with one of the words from the list below. The first one is done as an example.

    brains   trouble(s)
    proverbs work
    luck

1. Almost every language has its share of *proverbs*. (L-1)
2. That man has been sick, his house was robbed, and his wife lost her job. He has had his share of _____.
3. Today she lost her wallet twice and found it both times. She certainly has her share of _____.
4. He received A's in all his courses. He certainly must have his share of _____.
5. Cinderella's sisters never did their share of _____.

III. *share* (verb)
Fill in the blank in each sentence with one of the words from the list below. The first one is done as an example.

    office   certain feelings
    sandwich interest
    ideas

1. It is possible that all human beings share *certain feelings*. (L-2)
2. Three lawyers share the same crowded _____.
3. I see you forgot your lunch. Won't you share my _____ with me?
4. They share an _____ in mathematics.
5. The two friends share a lot of the same _____.

Answers to Vocabulary Study—Proverbs

I. 1. a
   2. b
   3. b
II. 1. proverbs
   2. trouble OR troubles
   3. luck
   4. brains
   5. work
III. 1. certain feelings
   2. office
   3. sandwich
   4. interest
   5. ideas

Folk Medicine

Discuss these key terms:

instinct	old wives' tales
herbs	myths

Listen to or read the summary below. Then try to answer the questions that follow:

SUMMARY

Contrary to what some people think, folk medicine is not a collection of medical old wives' tales. It is an ancient practice which helps to preserve the health of the body by using medicines taken from surrounding trees and plants. Materials for making folk medicines are found everywhere in the world. Man probably learned how to use the medicines by observing animals, which seem to have an instinct for knowing which plants and herbs will cure which illness.

QUESTIONS

1. What is folk medicine?
2. In the practice of folk medicine, where do materials for making medicines come from?
3. How did man learn to care for himself?

For suggested directions for doing these lessons see page 2 of this book.

Reading Text—Folk Medicine*

(1) Folk medicine reaches very far back in time. Nature opened the first drugstore. Primitive man and the animals depended on preventive use of its stock of plants and herbs to avoid disease and to maintain health and vigor. Because man and the animals were constantly on the move, Nature's drugstore had branches everywhere. Wherever in the world you were sick, you would find in the fields its medicines to cure you, its materials for curative herbal teas and ointments.

(2) . . . folk medicine adapts very old physiological and biochemical laws to the maintenance of health and vigor in the environmental conditions. . . . But there is no geographical limit on the laws, and their applications will work well in many environments.

(3) As with all . . . folk medicine from time immemorial, the ideal of . . . folk medicine is to condition the body in its entirety so that disease will not attack it. Now and then one finds people taking it for granted that "folk medicine" is a vague term for a collection of medical old wives' tales. It is inevitable that some myths would creep in along the way. For example, when I was a child, a string of Job's Tears—a species of grass having round, shiny grains imaginatively said to resemble the patient tears of the sorely tried Old Testament character—frequently were hung by a mother around the neck of her child "to help him cut his teeth." And of course all of us have heard of the supposedly magical, if smelly, powers of a little sack of asafoetida—the gum-resin substance with the garlicky odor—which, worn around the neck through the cold winter months, would surely repel sickness. In considering folk medicine, obviously witch-doctor myths should be separated from the genuine article.

(4) Our pioneer ancestors discovered the rudiments of their folk medicine in the healing plants sought out by animals suffering from alimentary disturbances, fever and wounds. By observing how animals cure themselves from disease, they learned how to keep themselves healthy by Nature's own methods.

(5) I have come to marvel at the instinct of animals to make use of natural laws for healing themselves. They know unerringly which herbs will cure what ills. Wild creatures first seek solitude and absolute relaxation, then they rely on the complete remedies of Nature—the medicine in plants and pure air. A bear grubbing for fern roots; a wild turkey compelling her babies in a rainy spell to eat leaves of the spice bush; an animal, bitten by a poisonous snake, confidently chewing snakeroot—all these are typical

examples. An animal with fever quickly hunts up an airy-shady place near water, there remaining quiet, eating nothing but drinking often until its health is recovered. On the other hand, an animal bedeviled by rheumatism finds a spot of hot sunlight and lies in it until the misery bakes out.

Listening Text—Folk Medicine

(1) Folk medicine maintains the health of the body by using medicines taken from surrounding plants and herbs. Since materials for making a medicine to cure a sickness can be found everywhere, one can practice folk medicine in any location of the world.

(2) The practice of folk medicine goes all the way back to the time of primitive man when both man and animal used plants and herbs in order to remain healthy. It is not uncommon, for example, to see an animal chew snakeroot after being bitten by a poisonous snake. Because animals seem to have this instinct for knowing which plants and herbs will cure what sickness, man probably learned how to care for himself by animal-watching.

(3) Man also learned other things from animals. He observed that wild creatures when sick remain quiet and rest, relying upon Nature's remedies for getting well—the medicine in plants and pure air. He saw that an animal with a fever could often be found resting in a cool place, eating nothing, and often drinking water until the fever was gone. He also watched animals afflicted with rheumatism remain in the hot sunlight waiting for the pain to be baked out.

(4) Some believe that folk medicine deals with a collection of old wives' tales concerning the medical treatment of the body. Stories are told about the powers of a certain vegetable material, which when hung around the neck, ensures the wearer of good health during the cold winter months. Such a story is simply a myth. It should be separated from the discussion of folk medicine.

Discussion—Folk Medicine

NOTES AND QUESTIONS ON DISCUSSION TAPE AND TEXT

This discussion is an informal conversation between two men. The subject is their grandmothers' health remedies. One of the men is from Ohio and the other is from Arkansas.

Some questions to explore:

How well educated are the speakers?

How well do they know each other?

Did they grow up in the city or in the country?

Study helps:

"had a thing about sassafras tea" means "had great faith in the value of sassafras tea"

"a legitimate part of folk medicine" means "real folk medicine, not an old wives' tale"

DISCUSSION

GARY: You know, Chuck, when I was a little boy I can remember being at my grandmother's house and having a sore throat and she had the idea that for my sore throat to be cured a black—I'll never forget it—a black elastic band should be put around my neck and I should wear this black elastic band around my neck the whole day.

CHUCK: Really?

GARY: Yes, it sounds funny, doesn't it?

CHUCK: Yeah, but—I guess—well my grandmother used to do that kind of thing, too.

GARY: Oh, really?

CHUCK: My grandmother had a thing about sassafras tea in the spring.

GARY: Oh, yeah. I've heard of it.

CHUCK: She would go out somewhere and actually dig up a root from a plant and—really—and she would boil it and it would make a kind of brown tea . . .

GARRY: With water.

CHUCK: Yeah, and it tastes like root beer drink tastes now. Maybe that's where root beer came from, but anyway my grandmother said that every spring you had to drink sassafras tea to thin your blood or something.

GARY: Oh, really?

CHUCK: And she really believed it.

GARY: Did it work?

CHUCK: Oh, I don't know if my blood was thinned or not, but I sort of liked the tea.

GARY: Yeah. Well, that practice sounds like it might have a little more scientific basis than the black elastic rubber band or black elastic band around somebody's neck for a sore throat. Maybe your grandmother was smarter than mine.

CHUCK: Oh, I doubt that. I guess all of this is a part of—what's it called—folk medicine?

GARY: Yes. Yes. Well, I think maybe your grandmother and her practice with the sassafras tea would qualify to be a legitimate part of folk medicine whereas my grandmother's method with the elastic band around one's neck—I don't think that should be part of folk medicine. It sounds more like a story, myth, to me with no scientific basis.

CHUCK: Hmm, hmm.

Speaking Activities—Folk Medicine

I

Answer on the basis of the Listening Text:

What might a practitioner of folk medicine advise you to do to remain healthy?

What do animals with a fever want to do?

What are some of the things that primitive man noticed about sick animals?

How can you keep from getting sick in the cold winter months—according to an old wives' tale? Do you believe this?

II

In the United States some people believe that this old saying is true: "Feed a fever, starve a cold" (that, is when you have a fever, eat as usual, but when you have a cold, don't eat anything). Other people believe that this is an old wives' tale. What do *you* do to help yourself when *you* have a fever or a cold?

Discuss other ailments and their treatments. Talk about whether the treatments are folk medicine or old wives' tales. For example:

stomach ache   hangover   hiccups
warts   diarrhea   toothache

You will be able to think of other ailments to discuss.

III

Do you think a doctor's prescription should be required to buy certain medicines? Why?

IV

Does night air affect health? Do you sleep with the window open or closed? Why?

V

Sometimes old wives' tales seem to work. For example, a wart may disappear after it has been rubbed with a raw potato and the potato has been buried. Or a person may feel better after he has drunk water from a certain spring. Can you explain these results?

VI

Dr. Jarvis states that man would be well advised to follow and pay attention to the behavior of animals. List some things which animals do which many people do already or might do, as far as health practices are concerned. For example, as warm weather grows near, the fur on animals decreases. Likewise as warm weather grows near, man discards heavy clothing in favor of lighter, cooler clothing.

VII

What customs or practices which are intended to prevent the spread of disease do you know about? How effective are these customs or practices?

Vocabulary Study—Folk Medicine

Find the words and phrases in the Reading Text which mean approximately the same as the words and phrases below. Write them in the blanks provided. (R-1 = Reading Text, paragraph 1, etc.)

The words and phrases below are listed in the order in which you will find the answers in the Reading Text. The first three are done as examples.

(R-1)

1. a supply _its stock_
2. plants, used for medical purposes _herbs_
3. energy _vigor_
4. salves _____

(R-2)

5. places _____

(R-3)

6. extending back beyond memory _____

7. strengthen _____

8. assuming that something is true
   without further investigation _____

9. unclear _____

10. superstitious beliefs _____

11. unavoidable _____

12. would develop as time passed by _____

13. severely tested _____

14. to help his teeth come
    through the gums _____

15. a man who attempts to cure sickness
    by the use of witchcraft _____

16. real folk medicine _____

(R-4)

17. basic principles _____

(R-5)

18. very impressed with _____

19. without error _____

20. privacy _____

21. digging _____

22. forcing _____

23. tormented _____

II. In the parentheses in each sentence below, write an expression, taken from the following list, that has the same meaning as the words that are in italics in the sentence. Put the expression in a form suitable to the sentence.

seek out
deal with

hunt up

depend on

rely on

The sentences below are similar to ones found in the reading and listening texts in the paragraphs indicated (for example, L-4 = Listening Text, paragraph 4; R-1 = Reading Text, paragraph 1). You can find the answers in these paragraphs.

1. **L-4** Some believe that folk medicine *has as its subject matter* (_____) a collection of old wives' tales.
2. **R-1** Primitive man and the animals *relied on* (_____) preventive use of plants and herbs to avoid disease.
3. **R-4** Animals suffering from alimentary disturbances *searched for and found* (_____) healing plants.
4. **R-5** Wild creatures *depend on* (_____) the complete remedies of nature.
5. **R-5** An animal with a fever *searches for and finds* (_____) an airy-shady place near the water.

Answers to Vocabulary Study—Folk Medicine

I. 1. its stock
  2. herbs
  3. vigor
  4. ointments
  5. environments
  6. from time immemorial
  7. condition
  8. taking it for granted
  9. vague
  10. old wives' tales
  11. inevitable
  12. would creep in along the way
  13. sorely tried
  14. to help him cut his teeth
  15. witch-doctor
  16. the genuine article
  17. rudiments

18. marvel at
19. unerringly
20. solitude
21. grubbing
22. compelling
23. bedeviled

II. 1. deals with
    2. depended on
    3. sought out
    4. rely on
    5. hunts up

Nonverbal Communication

"Maynard, your private face is showing."

Discuss these key terms:

social interaction

gestures

eye contact

physical distance between two speakers

verbal communication

Listen to or read the summary below. Then try to answer the questions that follow.

SUMMARY

Nonverbal communication is a form of social interaction. When two people are talking, their gestures and movements indicate something about the nature of their relationship. A steady gaze, a smile, the physical distance between the speaker and the listener are all said to carry a meaning of their own. We are going to talk about this form of behavior called nonverbal communication.

QUESTIONS

1. What is nonverbal communication?
2. What are some things which indicate the nature of the relationship of two people who are talking?
3. Name some examples of nonverbal communication not mentioned in the summary.

For suggested directions for doing these lessons see page 2 of this book.

Reading Text—Nonverbal Communication*

(1) Have you ever wondered why you sometimes take an almost immediate liking to a person you have just met? Or worried about why someone you were talking to suddenly became cool and distant? The chances are that it wasn't anything that was said but something that happened: a gesture, a movement, a raised eyebrow. Social scientists are now devoting considerable attention to "non-verbal communication," what happens when people get together, apart from their actual conversation.

(2) Anthropologist Erving Goffman of the University of Pennsylvania is involved in a continuing study of the way people behave in social interaction. He feels that supposedly irrelevant and insignificant behavior has real meaning in human communication.

(3) The closeness of two people when talking, movement towards and away from each other, and the amount of eye contact all reveal something about the nature of the relationship between the two individuals. We tend

*From the *Honolulu Advertiser*, Section D-2, Tuesday, March 18, 1969. Reprinted with permission.

to be only subliminally aware, if at all, of the various patterns and rituals of social behavior. We expect other people to act according to the same unwritten "rules" that we do, so much so that the manners and behavior of persons from another culture can be extremely mystifying and confusing.

(4) For example, North Americans tend to expect more physical distance between two speakers than do Latin Americans. Consequently, when the Latin American seems to be leaning too close, the North American complains of "pushiness." The Latin American, on the other hand, is puzzled and hurt by the withdrawing movements of the North American. Eye contact is one way of measuring the degree of intimacy between two speakers, although there are cultural variations in the meaning of eye contact. In the Middle East, for example, it is considered extremely provocative and flirtatious for a woman to let a man catch her eye, let alone return his gaze. Social psychologist Michael Argyle observes that there is more eye contact between people who like each other than those who are indifferent or hostile towards each other. And the longer the length of the gaze, the more likely it is that the listener is more interested in the person who is speaking, than the actual topic of conversation. Frequently looking down can indicate submissiveness, humility, or embarrassment. Looking away repeatedly may express boredom or dislike. Women tend to engage in more eye contact than men, especially when talking to other women.

(5) But too steady eye contact can be discomfitting at times. Most people become uncomfortable under the intense gaze of a stare. Desmond Morris, author of *The Naked Ape*, suggests that perhaps one reason that man becomes tense under the force of a stare is his biological antecedents: in apes, a stare signifies aggressiveness and hostility. The person who insistently affixes his eyes on our face is often more successful in arousing our ire than impressing us with his directness and sincerity.

(6) Similarly, the smile cannot always be interpreted as a sign of friendliness. The person who smiles almost constantly and with little apparent reason makes us uneasy. Even though he may believe that he is exuding friendliness, he may really seem overbearing and tense. In other animals, bared teeth are a warning gesture, a danger sign.

(7) Genuine warmth or interest is detected in the eyes, suggests Dr. Eckhard Hess of the University of Chicago, who believes that the pupils of the eyes can indicate emotion or interest. The dilated pupil tends to be associated with pleasant, satisfying experiences. That special sparkle in the lover's eyes need not be fantasy, for love and sexual excitement may dilate the pupil. It may be that when we feel that a person is "warm" and friendly, we are unconsciously reacting to our perception of his opened pupils.

(8) The next time you are at a party, take note of some of the silent messages being sent around you. Notice which persons seem to draw naturally together to speak, which others almost instinctively recoil and

avoid meeting each other's eyes. You may find that this silent language is much more fascinating than the actual conversation going on around you.

Listening Text—Nonverbal Communication

(1) I'd like to talk to you today about an article that appeared in the *Honolulu Advertiser*. The article was concerned with something called nonverbal communication. This is a phenomenon that scientists are now studying.

(2) Nonverbal communication has to do with gestures, movements, and closeness of two people when they are talking. The scientists say that these gestures, movements, and so forth have meaning which the words that the people are using do not carry.

(3) For example, the physical distance between two speakers can be important. North Americans often complain that South Americans are being "pushy" because they tend to stand close to the North American when speaking, whereas the South American often considers the North American to be "cold" or "distant" because he keeps a greater distance between himself and the person he is speaking to. In the Middle East it's considered flirtatious for a woman to allow a man to look her in the eye. This "eye contact" provides another example of what we're calling nonverbal communication. A social psychologist has observed that there is more eye contact between people who like each other than there is between poeple who don't like each other. The length of time that the person whom you are speaking to looks at your eyes indicates the amount of interest he has in you rather than the amount of interest he has in the thing you are talking about.

(4) On the other hand, too long a gaze can be discomfiting. Most people become uncomfortable when they're stared at. The eyes apparently play a great part in nonverbal communication. Frequently looking down can indicate submissiveness, humility, or embarrassment, or even boredom or dislike. Genuine warmth or interest can often be seen in the eyes. One scientist suggests that pleasant, satisfying experiences tend to make the pupils of the eyes grow larger. Sometimes when we feel that a person is being "warm" or "friendly" it is possible that we are reacting to a form of nonverbal communication—his opened pupils.

(5) We do not always consider a smile to be a sign of friendliness. Someone who is always smiling, and with little apparent reason, often makes us feel uneasy.

(6) Keep in mind what we've said about nonverbal communication, and the next time you're at a party try to notice which persons seem to draw close together when speaking—which persons seem to try to stay further apart or even to avoid each other. You may find this silent language, which

we've called nonverbal communication, very interesting and even fascinating.

Discussion—Nonverbal Communication

NOTES AND QUESTIONS ON DISCUSSION TAPE AND TEXT

Art is reading the newspaper. Craig enters the room and would like to talk, but Art wants to continue reading the paper. Both men are in college. Craig is a native of Hawaii and Art of New Jersey.

Some questions to explore:

How well do the speakers know each other?
How long has it been since the two speakers have talked with each other?
Is Art angry with Craig?
Is Craig a talkative person?

Study helps:

The Advertiser is the name of a daily newspaper.

DISCUSSION

CRAIG: Hi, see you're reading the newspaper.
ART: Uh-huh.
CRAIG: Looks like *The Advertiser*.
ART: Mmm.
CRAIG: Looks pretty interesting.
ART: Mmm. Uh.
CRAIG: Did you go to school today?
ART: Huh-uh!
CRAIG: What're you reading?
ART: _____
CRAIG: Well, what're you reading?
ART: Huh?
CRAIG: What're you reading there in that article?
ART: Oh, uhm, this is about nonverbal communication.
CRAIG: Nonverbal communication? What's that?

ART: Well that's a way of communicating with people but without using words. For example, gestures and movements. Uh, yesterday something happened that is a good illustration of it. My friend and I were going to a restaurant and we wanted to park our car at the restaurant's parking lot. The attendant motioned to us to park at a certain stall but I thought it was kind of inconvenient—there was one much closer—so without saying anything I pointed at the other stall, indicating that I'd like to park at that one, but the attendant motioned with his hand "No," and pointed at the first one again indicating that I should park there. I nodded and parked my car there. No, no words had passed between us, and yet we understood each other.

CRAIG: Oh, so that's nonverbal communication.

ART: Uh-huh.

Speaking Activities—Nonverbal Communication

I

Answer on the basis of the Listening Text:

What might a boy in the Middle East think if a girl allowed him to look her in the eye?

What advice about nonverbal communication would you give to a North American who was visiting South America?

What kind of physical distance do South Americans prefer?

What might you expect of a person who looks down frequently?

II

For the first few class meetings be prepared to report on gestures and other forms of nonverbal communication you have seen used when people are talking (in the cafeteria, at home, during a meeting, in an elevator, on television, on the telephone, in traffic, at the airport, etc.).

III

Working with at least one other person, try to think of American gestures—body movements—that have the same meaning as the words that follow.

1. No.
2. Yes.
3. Wow, she really has a good figure.
4. Stop.
5. I'm cold.

6. A-OK.
7. I don't know.
8. Good luck.
9. What time is it?
10. I'm quoting.

IV

Do you feel that nonverbal communication is less important, equally as important, or more important than verbal communication? (Verbal communication = speech and writing).

V

Discuss misunderstandings that have happened because of a misinterpretation of nonverbal communication. For example, an American woman was visiting in Thailand and left her purse in a shop. The shopkeeper hurried out to call the lady back and used the Thai sign for "come here" but the American lady showed her misinterpretation by raising her hand and saying, "Bye, bye."

VI

When would it be appropriate to use the gestures listed in Speaking Activity III? Consider the relationship between the speakers (how well they know each other, their ages, their sex) and the situation (formal, informal, number of people present).

Vocabulary Study—Nonverbal Communication

I. In each of the blanks in the sentences below, write one of the following words, *but in a form that fits the sentence.*

appear	(Verb)	(Adjective)
submit	(Verb)	(Noun)
humble	(Adjective)	(Noun)
perceive	(Verb)	(Noun)
provoke	(Verb)	(Noun)
intimate	(Adjective)	(Noun)
mystery	(Noun)	(Participial Adjective)

The first part of speech after each word indicates its part of speech in the list; the second part of speech indicates how it should be used in the sentence below.

The sentences are copied from the texts, and you can check the text, if you want to, to find the answers. L-2 = Listening Text, paragraph 2; R-4 = Reading Text, paragraph 4, and so forth.

The first blank is filled in as an example.

1. **(R-3)** . . . the manners and behavior of persons from another culture can be extremely *mystifying* and confusing.

2. **(R-4)** Eye contact is one way of measuring the degree of _____ between two speakers. . . .

3. **(R-4)** Frequently looking down can indicate _____, _____, or embarrassment.

4. **(R-4)** In the Middle East it is considered extremely _____ and flirtatious for a woman to let a man catch her eye.

5. **(R-6)** The person who smiles constantly and with little _____ reason makes us uneasy.

6. **(R-7)** It may be that when we feel that a person is "warm" and friendly, we are unconsciously reacting to our _____ of his opened pupils.

II. In the sentences below, fill in the blanks with the prefix that is needed to make the word negative. The first blank is filled as an example.

1. **(R-2)** Goffman feels that supposedly *ir* relevant and _____ significant behavior has real meaning in human communication.

2. **(R-3)** We expect other people to act according to the same _____ written "rules" that we do.

3. **(R-4)** Looking away repeatedly may express boredom or _____ like.

4. **(L-4)** Most people become _____ comfortable when they're stared at.

5. **(L-6)** Keep in mind what we've said about _____ verbal communication.

III. The reading and listening texts talk about *physical* distance. In English, words that have to do with space are also used to express emotional distance (or closeness).

Here are some examples of some common expressions:

to be close to someone
to grow apart from someone
to have a far-away look in one's eyes

to keep someone at arm's length
to look up to someone
to look down on someone

Can you fill in the blanks in the sentences below with the appropriate forms of the above expressions?

1. They have been _____ for quite some time. They hardly ever see each other any more.

2. He had such a _____ in his eyes that I'm sure he didn't hear a word that was said.

3. Those two sisters are very _____ to each other.

4. He _____ to his older brother. He really admires him.

5. If I didn't keep her at _____, she would be asking me for favors all the time.

6. You shouldn't _____ on him. He's an admirable person.

IV. The following sentences use the adjective "close" in various ways. Match the meanings on the right with the sentences on the left by placing the appropriate letters in the parentheses.

(   ) 1. That race was *close*.
(   ) 2. He kept a *close* watch on the stock market.
(   ) 3. The room is getting *close*.
(   ) 4. She wore a *close*-fitting dress.
(   ) 5. She is very *close-mouthed* about her plans.
(   ) 6. He's very *close* to his degree.
(   ) 7. He's very *close* with his money.

A. tight
B. stuffy
C. secretive
D. stingy
E. careful and constant
F. near
G. decided by a narrow margin

Answers to Vocabulary Study—Nonverbal Communication

I. 1. mystifying
   2. intimacy
   3. submissiveness, humility
   4. provocative
   5. apparent
   6. perception

II. 1. irrelevant, insignificant
   2. unwritten
   3. dislike

    4. uncomfortable

    5. nonverbal

III. 1. growing apart

    2. far-away look

    3. close

    4. looks up

    5. arm's length

    6. look down

IV. 1. G

    2. E

    3. B

    4. A

    5. C

    6. F

    7. D or A

Intelligence

THROUGH HISTORY WITH J. WESLEY SMITH

"No, I didn't commit any crime—they just gave me an aptitude test."

Preview

Discuss these key terms:

IQ tests

achievement in school

stupid

bright

Listen to or read the summary below. Then try to answer the questions that follow:

SUMMARY

Intelligence is actually a way of living and behaving. IQ tests and achievement in school are only indicators of intelligence. Therefore, in order to test intelligence, one must also find out how an individual would act in new situations. "Bright" children and "not-bright" children are two different kinds of people. They have different ways of looking at life and different ways of acting. Except for those children who are born with problems, no child is born stupid. During the first three years of life all children learn and grow intellectually. The child's ability to learn, however, is destroyed in most homes and in the school.

QUESTIONS

1. What is intelligence?
2. What are two indicators of intelligence?
3. How can intelligence be tested?
4. Are bright children and not-bright children different kinds of people?
5. Is any child born stupid?
6. When do all children grow intellectually?
7. Where is the child's ability to learn destroyed?

For suggested directions for doing these lessons see page 2 of this book.

Reading Text—Intelligence*

(1) When we talk about intelligence, we do not mean the ability to get a good score on a certain kind of test, or even the ability to do well in school. These are at best only indicators of something larger, deeper, and far more important. By intelligence we mean a style of life, a way of behaving in various situations, and particularly in new, strange and perplexing situations. The true test of intelligence is not how much we know how to do, but how we behave when we don't know what to do.

(2) The intelligent person, young or old, meeting a new situation or problem, opens himself up to it; he tries to take in with mind and senses everything he can about it; he thinks about *it*, instead of about himself or what it might cause to happen to him; he grapples with it boldly, imaginatively, resourcefully, and if not confidently at least hopefully: if he fails to master it, he looks without shame or fear at his mistakes and learns what he can from them. This is intelligence. Clearly its roots lie in a certain feeling about life, and one's self with respect to life. Just as clearly, unintelligence is not what most psychologists seem to suppose, the same thing as intelligence, only less of it. It is an entirely different style of behavior, arising out of an entirely different set of attitudes.

(3) Years of watching and comparing bright children and the not-

*From the book *How Children Fail* by John Holt. Copyright ©, 1964 by Pitman Publishing Corporation. Reprinted by permission of Pitman Publishing Corp.

bright, or less bright, have shown that they are very different kinds of people. The bright child is curious about life and reality, eager to get in touch with it, embrace it, unite himself with it. There is no wall, no barrier between him and life. The dull child is far less curious, far less interested in what goes on and what is real, more inclined to live in worlds of fantasy. The bright child likes to experiment, to try things out. He lives by the maxim that there is more than one way to skin a cat. If he can't do something one way, he'll try another. The dull child is usually afraid to try at all. It takes a great deal of urging to get him to try even once; if that try fails, he is through. . . .

(4) Nobody starts off stupid. Hardly an adult in a thousand, or ten thousand, could in any three years of his life learn as much, grow as much in his understanding of the world around him, as every infant learns and grows in his first three years. But what happens, as we get older, to this extraordinary capacity for learning and intellectual growth?

(5) What happens is that it is destroyed, and more than by any other one thing, by the process that we misname education—a process that goes on in most homes and schools.

Listening Text—Intelligence

(1) When a person talks about intelligence, he isn't thinking just of schoolwork or of scores on IQ tests. Of course, these things *do* show intelligence, but they're only sort of indicators of real intelligence. Intelligence is a way of living and behaving, especially in a new or upsetting situation. If we actually want to test intelligence, we need to find out how a person acts when he really doesn't know what to do.

(2) For instance, when in a new situation, an intelligent person thinks about the situation, not about himself or what might happen to him. He tries to find out all he can, and then he goes right ahead and tries to do something about it. He probably isn't sure how it will all work out, but at least he tries. And, if he can't make things work out right, he doesn't feel ashamed that he failed; he just tries to learn from his mistakes. An intelligent person, even if he's very young, has a special outlook on life, a special feeling about life, and how he fits into it.

(3) English doesn't seem to have a good word for the opposite of intelligent, but we can use "unintelligent." This "unintelligence" isn't just a smaller amount of intelligence. It's a lot different: it's a different way of looking at life and also a different way of acting.

(4) If you look at children, you'll see a big difference between what we call "bright" children and "not-bright" children. They are actually two different *kinds* of people, not just the same kind with different amounts of intelligence. For example, the bright child really wants to find out about life—he tries to get in touch with everything around him. But, the dull

child sticks more to himself and his own dream-world; he seems to have a wall between him and life in general.

(5) When the bright child gets into trouble, he experiments—he keeps on trying. Somehow he feels there's more than one way to skin a cat, so he keeps trying until he finds a way that works. But the dull child probably doesn't even try at all. You have to urge him and push him to get him to try even once, and then if he fails, he won't try again.

(6) How come some children turn out dull? Except for the few who are born with problems, nobody starts off stupid. Just look at how much a child learns in the first three years of his life! Yet out of a group of, say, 10,000 adults, there's hardly anyone who could increase his understanding of the world around him *that* much in only three years. What happens to us as we grow older? What happens to our ability to learn—to grow intellectually?

(7) This ability gets destroyed—and it's destroyed mostly by the process we call education. It gets destroyed in most of our homes and schools, right in the places where most education is supposed to take place.

Discussion—Intelligence

NOTES AND QUESTIONS ON DISCUSSION TAPE AND TEXT

Two friends are talking about the Reading Text on Intelligence. Carolyn is a native of Texas and Larry is from Arkansas. Note the southern accent. You should have no trouble understanding it.

Some questions to explore:

What are the educational backgrounds of the speakers?
Is this a formal or an informal conversation?
Are Larry and Carolyn old friends or have they just met?

Study helps:

"more than one way to skin a cat" means "more than one way to do a job or solve a problem"
"seems to imply" means "seems to suggest"
"the way I interpret" means "the way I understand"
"born deficient" means "born lacking in mental ability"

DISCUSSION

LARRY: What do you feel are Mr. Holt's major points in this article?
CAROLYN: Well, first of all, I think one of his major points is his

definition of intelligence. He says that intelligence is a way of behaving, the way people react to new situations, the way they adjust to a new problem.

LARRY: Do you think we might find another word—instead of using intelligence—another word would be better suited here?

CAROLYN: Yes, I do. Maybe the word—ah—performance or capabilities —either one of those words to me would describe better—ah—the way he feels intelligence is.

LARRY: Yes. Me too. Another thing, a question I have is how he divides the world into two groups, two kinds of people he says, rather than having one kind with different amounts of intelligence he says there are two different kinds of people. I'm not really too clear on that.

CAROLYN: It does seem kind of confusing, but I think he is trying to say that there's a bright child and a dull child. The bright child will face a new problem, he will try many solutions, he will be aware of the world around him. If one thing fails, he will try another way of solving it. He will know that there is more than one way to skin a cat, while the dull person easily gives up after one failure. He seems to be in a world of his own, and he is not aware of things around him.

LARRY: But Mr. Holt seems to imply that this dull person or this dull child is created at the school or that what . . . the way I interpret what he's saying. . . . Because he does say that unless, except for those few exceptions where we are born deficient or mentally retarded, no one is born dull or not bright. Is that your impression?

CAROLYN: Yes, he seems to feel that education is what has stifled or what has destroyed the ability that a person is born with. I think this would be a good topic for discussion: How the schools or how education destroys the ability of a person to grow intellectually, to—the ability to face new problems, new situations.

Speaking Activities—Intelligence

I

Answer on the basis of the Listening Text:

What does Holt (the author of the Reading Text) think intelligence is?

Is anything mentioned about IQ tests? What?

What does a bright child do when he gets into trouble?

According to the author, what makes children dull?

What might you advise a person in a strange situation to do?

II

Holt says that the infant, during his first three years, learns more than he will ever learn in any three years after that. In other words, the infant grows more intellectually during his first three years than the average adult does in any three years. Do you agree with Holt? Why?

III

Do you feel more intelligent with some people than with others? If so, how do you explain this feeling?

IV

Before a child begins elementary school in your country, what sort of education does he receive? Is this education mostly up to the mother, the grandmother, a nursery school teacher, a kindergarten teacher, a combination of these? Does this pre-school education contribute to "intelligence," in Holt's terms? What are its good points? What are its weak points?

V

Talk about the ways that education can influence intellectual growth. Remember, Holt believes that present methods of education often make students stupid rather than intelligent. Do you agree?

VI

Think of a famous, living person, who you think is intelligent. Without his name, tell *why* you think he is intelligent. Answer any questions your classmates may have and then see if they can guess who the person is.

Vocabulary Study—Intelligence

I. In each set of sentences below, fill in the blanks with the appropriate form of the word in parentheses. For example, in the first set of sentences, fill in the blanks with the appropriate forms of *perplex*—for example, *perplexing, perplexed.*

   1. (perplex) He is _____. The situation is _____. He is in a _____ situation. A _____ child needs to experiment.

2. (upset)   People sometimes get _____. Things sometimes _____ them. Some situations are very
   _____.

3. (interest)   Bright children are _____ in many things.
   They find life _____. They like _____ situations. They are _____ in _____ situations.

II. Read the sentences below and decide, for each sentence, whether
both *strange* and *curious* could fit into the blank or whether only
curious fits. Can you figure out what the two meanings of *curious*
are?

   strange **(R-1)**   curious **(R-3)**

   1. Her _____ analysis of the book surprised him.
   2. He cast a _____ look around the room.
   3. She is wearing a _____ combination of colors.
   4. I think something is wrong because he gave me a very
      _____ look.
   5. Children are naturally _____ about the world around
      them.
   6. He has many _____ habits.

III. Read the sentences below and decide for each sentence, whether
both *strangely* and *curiously* could fit into the blank or whether
only *curiously* fits.

   1. They _____ awaited the news.
   2. I wonder why he is acting so _____.
   3. _____, I forgot to bring a pencil to the examination.
   4. She looked through the book _____.
   5. They sat there _____, wondering what was expected
      of them.
   6. _____ enough, she used his exact words, though she
      hadn't heard him say them.

Answers to Vocabulary Study—Intelligence

I. 1. perplexed, perplexing, perplexing, perplexed
   2. upset, upset, upsetting, upsetting
   3. interested, interesting, interesting, interested, interesting

II. 1. strange, curious
   2. strange, curious
   3. strange, curious

    4. strange, curious

    5. curious

    6. strange, curious

NOTE: *curious* sometimes means "odd or different" and sometimes "inquisitive." Strange means "odd or different."

III. 1. curiously

    2. strangely, curiously

    3. strangely, curiously

    4. curiously

    5. curiously

    6. strangely, curiously

Propaganda

the small society   **by Brickman**

HOO-BOY!

I'M ONE OF THE PEOPLE WHO CAN BE FOOLED SOME OF THE TIME —

7-18

Washington Star Syndicate, Inc.

BRICKMAN

Preview

Discuss these key terms:

propaganda techniques
persuasion
propaganda analyst

Listen to or read the summary below. Then try to answer the questions that follow:

SUMMARY

Propaganda is all around us. Anyone trying to persuade someone else to do something uses propaganda techniques. A baby just by crying forces the people around him to please him. Yet the baby does not respond very well to his family's efforts to control him. A baby often wants things that his parents do not want to give him. The parents also often try to do what they think is best for the baby, but the baby wants something else done. Therefore, both the parents and the baby try to persuade each other. If a child repeatedly finds his parents to be both wise and unselfish, he'll believe that what they say is best. However, occasionally even the best parent makes mistakes. The problem for the child is to discover just when he can trust his parents' judgment.

QUESTIONS

1. Who uses propaganda techniques?
2. Do a baby and his parents always want the same thing?
3. What is it that a child has to discover?
4. Is propaganda bad?

For suggested directions for doing these lessons see page 2 of this book.

Reading Text—Propaganda*

(1) Persuasive efforts are labelled *propagandistic* when someone judges that the action which is the goal of the persuasive effort will be advantageous to the persuader but not in the best interests of the persuadee. . . .

(2) The cries of infancy are expressive of infant needs and, in addition, are wonderfully persuasive. Totally dependent on the actions of others, the infant has not the strength to constrain others to do his will. But he is set down in the midst of a community intent on learning what he needs and satisfying him. . . .

(3) The infant himself is not very responsive to persuasive efforts but is, nevertheless, subjected to them from the very beginning. . ∴. He is moved and put to bed by the direct application of force but he cannot be made to eat or sleep or smile. These greatly desired reactions cannot be forced and an effort is made to wheedle them from him. He reigns as an absolute monarch. His casual utterances are studied so that he may be pleased. All about him, supplicants smile and entreat him to accept what is offered. . . .

(4) We may assume that parents identify their own interests with what is good for the child rather than with his desires. In addition, adults have interests of their own which are only vaguely and, perhaps, by rationaliza-tion, connected with the infant's best interests but which definitely conflict with his desires. Father does not want his watch broken and mother is too tired to carry a baby around by the hour. So there occurs a diversion of interests from the parental point of view and also from the child's point of view and consequently the opportunity for propaganda warfare.

(5) When father tastes baby's food and smacks his lips over it baby may be led to taste. If the taste is pretty bad a propaganda analyst is born. When this persuasive device is used again he will feel himself to be the object of propagandistic effort. However, father is no subjective propagandist. He

believes that he is acting in the best interests of the child. Where parents repeatedly prove to be both wise and unselfish we may suppose that a child will not identify their persuasive efforts as propagandistic. He will feel their interests are identical with his own but that they are better able to calculate these interests than he is. They know that fire burns, knives are sharp, and that cats will scratch. He can rely on them as an information source that is devoted to his welfare.

(6) However, it is a rare parent who never tries to persuade a child to do something solely for the sake of parental comfort. Most parents are occasionally conscious propagandists trying to talk a boy out of a trip to the zoo on Sunday. So children discover that parents are not invariably selfless. It is a rare parent who is not sometimes proved wrong. Timid mothers overestimate the probability that dogs will bite and that cats will scratch, and children find that out. Consequently most parents are regarded as often reliable informers but as occasional propagandists. The trick is to discover when they are making propaganda.

Listening Text—Propaganda

(1) Have you ever thought how much we use propaganda, or are influenced by propaganda every day? Any time you try to persuade someone to do something that is to your advantage, you are practicing propaganda techniques—especially if it is not in the best interests of the person you're trying to influence.

(2) A baby's cries express his needs; they are also very persuasive! Even though the baby doesn't have the physical strength to force others to do what he wants done, he can often persuade them to please him. In fact, the community he lives in (his family) spends a lot of time learning what he needs and how to make him happy.

(3) On the other hand, the baby doesn't respond very well to his family's persuasive efforts. They can put him in bed or in front of food, but they can't make him sleep, eat, or smile. *He* is in control. They can only try to coax a smile or word from him.

(4) Parents seem to feel that what is good for them is also good for the child. Often the interests of the adults are definitely in conflict with the desires of the baby. Father doesn't want his watch broken, so baby can't play with it; mother is too tired to carry baby around by the hour, so he has to lie in his crib. This difference in baby's desires and parents' interests sets things up for propaganda warfare within the home.

(5) Father, trying to feed baby, tastes the strained carrots (ugh!), smacks his lips, and shoves the spoon at baby. Baby tries it (a victim of father's propaganda?). If the taste is pretty bad, a propaganda analyst is born; probably next time baby will think twice before believing father's smacking

lips. Father doesn't see himself as a propagandist; he just believes he is doing what is best for the baby.

(6) If the child repeatedly finds his parents to be both wise and unselfish, he probably won't think that their persuasive efforts are propagandistic. He will feel that their interests are identical with his, but somehow that they are better able to figure out what these interests actually are. When they say that fire burns, knives cut, and cats scratch, he will believe them if he has learned in the past to respect their judgment.

(7) However, it is a rare parent who doesn't occasionally try to persuade a child to do something purely because it helps the parent. Most parents are conscious propagandists when they're trying to talk junior out of a Sunday trip to the zoo—especially if they're tired. Children *do* discover that parents are sometimes selfish. Besides, even a sincere parent is occasionally proved wrong. For instance, timid mothers often feel that all dogs bite and all cats scratch—but their children find out that many don't. All children eventually learn that although their parents are often reliable, these same parents are also occasionally propagandists. The problem for the child is to figure out just when they are making propaganda.

Discussion—Propaganda

NOTES AND QUESTIONS ON DISCUSSION TAPE AND TEXT

The speakers in this conversation are two university graduate students. The woman is from Michigan and the man is from Iowa.

Some questions to explore:

Is this the beginning or the middle of the conversation?

Are the speakers close friends?

Are they completely relaxed and at ease?

What do you think is the reason for this discussion?

Study helps:

"discriminate" means "to see the difference between what is propaganda and what is not propaganda"

"to take propaganda with a grain of salt" means "to listen to propaganda, but without believing everything that is said"

"on his own" means doing something "without expecting any reward or payment"

DISCUSSION

HARVEY: Well, I suppose, suppose the biggest trouble is that most propaganda is distorted. It's not the whole truth. You just get somebody's—

FRANCES: Yes, you just get some of it, and some of it is good and some of it is bad.

HARVEY: Yeah.

FRANCES: And so you have to just sort of be careful, I guess.

HARVEY: You have to learn to—

FRANCES: An you have s———

HARVEY: Well, yeah—you have to learn to discriminate, or—

FRANCES: Yeah, I guess maybe that's the term—discriminate—learn to take propaganda with a grain of salt, I suppose.

HARVEY: Yeah, it's a—you've got a—you know, I think it's easier to, uh, judge propaganda if you know the motives, or if you can figure out the motive behind it. If it's to sell, well then you, you'll be more suspicious, you know. If the guy's, uh, goes on about somebody's health, or this, this, new thing will make you live longer, well then— uh, if he's *selling* the new thing, then I'm suspicious. If he's *not* selling it, and, you know, just on his own recommending something he heard or knows and such, well that's different. But, uh—

FRANCES: Of course, a lot of these companies, you know, that, that uh, are introducing new products, they'll, they'll, send a sample, sample of these products to the home. Of course that, you know, you can find out for yourself whether the propaganda's—uh, there's any that—any truth to the—propaganda that they're spreading concerning their product.

HARVEY: Yeah, uh—in a culture where you've got so many different uhm, people making almost the same thing, it's a—I find it a real problem—to, to figure out what's good.

FRANCES: You really don't know which one you're, you want or you really don't know if they're all the same, if one is just as good as the other, or whether maybe one *is* better than the other. So you just, you just have to sort of learn to discriminate, I suppose.

HARVEY: And in the meantime, you lose a lot of money on, uh, testing their products, if you're like me.

Speaking Activities—Propaganda

I

Answer on the basis of the Listening Text:

What can a baby persuade his parents to do?
What are some things that parents cannot make a baby do?

What are some of the propaganda efforts the author has seen parents
   make?
What are some things that are good for a child to find out?

                                                                    II

For the next few class meetings be prepared to report on (1) recent
attempts made to persuade *you* to do something, and (2) recent attempts
you have made to persuade *someone else* to do something.

                                                                    III

Can you remember what means of persuasion you used with your
parents when you were a child to get what you wanted? Discuss.

                                                                    IV

Talk about the propaganda techniques that advertisers use. What are
some of the human weaknesses that they take advantage of? How do they
do this?

                                                                    V

Some people use certain names for races, political parties, religions,
and so forth, that express dislike. Mention some names like this that you
have heard and talk about who would use them and when. Here are two
examples of such names: Yankee, imperialist.

                                                                    VI

What propaganda techniques do governments use to try to create a
favorable impression?

Vocabulary Study—Propaganda

I. *make* In four of the sentences below, "make" means "cause
   (someone) to be" or "cause (someone) to." In one sentence it
   means "create." Draw a circle around each *make* that means
   "cause (someone) to be" or "cause (someone) to."
   1. People try to *make* babies happy.
   2. The family can't always *make* the baby smile.

3. Carrying a baby around by the hour *makes* the mother tired.

4. Sometimes parents *make* propaganda.

5. They tried to *make* the baby eat.

II. *feel*   In four of the sentences below, *feel* means "think." In one sentence it means "be." Draw a circle around each *feel* that means "think."

1. Parents *feel* that what is good for them is also good for the child.

2. He will *feel* himself to be the object of a propagandistic effort.

3. The mother may *feel* too tired to carry the baby around by the hour.

4. Mothers sometimes *feel* that all dogs bite and all cats scratch.

5 The child will *feel* that his parent's interests are identical with his.

III. *believe*   In four of the sentences below, *believe* means "think." In one sentence it means "accept the beliefs of." Draw a circle around each *believe* that means "think."

1. Parents *believe* that what is good for them is also good for the child.

2. The child will *believe* his parents if he has learned to respect their judgment.

3. The parent *believes* that he is acting in the best interest of the child.

4. Father *believes* that strained carrots are good for the baby.

5. Most children *believe* their parents to be reliable most of the time.

IV. *want*   In four of the sentences below, *want* means "wish." In one sentence it means "covet," that is, "wish to possess." Draw a circle around each *want* that means "wish."

1. Father does not *want* his watch broken.

2. He *wants* something done.

3. Father *wants* the baby to eat the strained carrots.

4. Parents don't always *want* to take their children to the zoo.

5. The child *wants* his father's watch.

V. *find*   In four of the sentences below *find* refers to a mental discovery. In one sentence it refers to a physical discovery. Draw a circle around each *find* that refers to a mental discovery.

1. The baby *found* a watch to play with.

2. A child usually *finds* his parents to be both wise and unselfish.

3. The boy *found* that he didn't like strained carrots.

4. Sometimes parents *find* selfish reasons for not doing what the child wants.

5. Have you *found* how to make a baby happy?

Answers to Vocabulary Study—Propaganda

   I. Draw circles around *make* in sentences 1, 2, 3, 5.

  II. Draw circles around *feel* in sentences 1, 2, 4, 5.

 III. Draw circles around *believe* in sentences 1, 3, 4, 5.

 IV. Draw circles around *want* in sentences 1, 2, 3, 4.

  V. Draw circles around *find* in sentences 2, 3, 4, 5.

Words in Context

Discuss these key terms:

context
define
synonym
comparison
contrast
clue

Listen to or read the summary below. Then try to answer the questions that follow:

SUMMARY

There are a number of ways to find out the meaning of a new word. The quickest way is to get the meaning from the context. Sometimes the text contains a defining synonym. Other times a comparison or contrast is made that helps with the meaning. Look for meaning clues in the context before you look elsewhere.

QUESTIONS

1. What is the quickest way to find out the meaning of a new word?
2. What is a "defining synonym"?
3. Why do you think the dictionary is not mentioned in the summary above?

For suggested directions for doing these lessons see page 2 of this book.

Reading Text—Words in Context*

(1) What do you do when you encounter a word that is not familiar? Do you stop to look it up, do you try to analyze its parts, or do you look for clues in the way the word is used in its settings or surroundings?

(2) There are several methods that may be used in unlocking the meaning of unfamiliar words. But the quickest and most practical approach is knowing how to use the context, or the words around the unknown word, to unlock its meaning. This method is called using context clues or "word clues."

(3) You may say, "Why not look up all words in a dictionary?" . . . There are many times a dictionary will not be available. Even if you're reading with a dictionary near at hand, you don't want to stop every few minutes to look up a word. The chain of thought would be interrupted so often that you would lose much of the pleasure and profit in your reading.

(4) Let's look at some of the ways we can get the meaning of a word from context without looking it up in the dictionary.

(5) 1. One way to use context clues is to look for a *synonym* or a word that has the same meaning. Sometimes a writer or a speaker will give a synonym for an unfamiliar word just to make sure that we understand it. For example, look at this sentence:

"When an atom undergoes fission or splitting, a tremendous amount of energy is released."

In this case, the author thought that you might not know the meaning of *fission,* so he provided a synonym—*splitting.*

(6) 2. At other times, the context may give us a fairly good meaning of a word by telling what it is like or even what it is not like. We might call these clues of similarities or differences. Do you know what *opacity* means? See if you can figure out its meaning from these two sentences:

"The opacity of various materials differs greatly. We know, for example, that transparent substances, such as air, glass, and water, have almost no opacity. Light passes directly through them."

(7) Now you know that *opacity* means something that is different from air, glass, and water, or something that is not clear or transparent. When

*From *EDL Word Clues* by Stanford E. Taylor, Helen Frackenpohl, Arthur S. McDonald, Nancy Joline, New York: Educational Developmental Laboratories, Division of McGraw-Hill Book Company, 1961, Introduction. Reprinted by permission.

materials are clear or transparent and light passes through them easily, they are said to have no *opacity*. Therefore, you can reason that *opacity* must mean "a blocking of light."

(8) When you cannot use context clues, you must use the dictionary. But even then you will need to use context clues in order to select the appropriate dictionary definition. The dictionary might give you the generally accepted meaning or perhaps a number of different meanings. It is up to you to choose the correct meaning and adapt it to the context with which you are working.

Listening Text—Words in Context

(1) What do you do when you run across a word that you don't know? Do you grab a dictionary? Do you see if the word has any parts you already know? Do you look for some clues to what it means by the way it fits into its surroundings or context?

(2) The quickest way to figure out the meaning of a new word is to look at its setting in the sentence or paragraph where you find it. Using a dictionary takes too long—besides, you lose the train of thought of the sentences when you have to go to the dictionary.

(3) Let's figure out some ways to use the context of a word to get its meaning.

(4) Some speakers and writers are pretty good at guessing which of their words won't be understood right off, so they often give the synonym of a new word. How about this sentence?

(5) "When an atom undergoes fission or splitting, a tremendous amount of energy is released."

(6) The speaker here figured that "fission" might be a new word to someone, so he gave a synonym for it when he said "an atom undergoes fission or splitting . . ." What does fission mean? Why, splitting, of course. Without looking up fission, you know it means splitting—you got the meaning from the context.

(7) Sometimes you'll have to look for clues from similarities or differences pointed out by the context—you are told what something is like or not like. For example, do you know what "opacity" means? Could you figure it out from these two sentences?

(8) "The opacity of various materials differs greatly. We know, for example, that transparent substances, such as air, glass, and water, have almost no opacity. Light passes directly through them."

(9) You can tell from this that "opacity" means something that air, glass, and water don't have. When something is transparent or clear—when light passes through it easily—you say it doesn't have opacity. So "opacity" must mean "a stopping, or blocking of light."

(10) Of course looking for either synonyms or explanations of new words is not the only way to figure out meaning from context, but *do* use these two. I hope that before you reach for a dictionary or before you ask "what do you mean?", you'll make a guess from the context.

Discussion—Words in Context

NOTES AND QUESTIONS ON DISCUSSION TAPE AND TEXT

In this conversation the woman is from the western part of the United States and the man is from the Midwest. The segment on the tape is taken from a longer conversation.

Some questions to explore:

Is this a formal or an informal conversation?
What are the educational backgrounds of the speakers?
Do you think the speakers are good friends?
How old do you think the speakers are?

Study helps:

Notice that at one time *really* occurs as a question ("Really?"), and at another time as a comment ("Really!")

DISCUSSION

HARVEY: When you're reading a textbook, how often do you look in the dictionary?

CAROLE: Oh, not very often, I don't think.

HARVEY: Even in the textbook?

CAROLE: Oh, well, it'd depend—you know, if it was really a, a technical word, or something like that—something which I really couldn't understand any other way, I'd probably look it up. But, uh—probably not if I was just reading along. It would probably take me too long.

HARVEY: Yeah, I think so. You know, ah, when I'm reading a newspaper, *Newsweek*, or a novel, I don't think I've ever looked up a word. I don't think I've ever taken a dictionary. How about you?

CAROLE: I don't even have one, as a matter of fact.

HARVEY: Really?

CAROLE: Really! I went all through college without buying a dictionary. The times that I had to look up something which was a technical word or something, I made it a point to go to the uh, to the uh . . .

HARVEY: To the library?

CAROLE: Library or something and find the dictionary.

HARVEY: Well, where'd you find out the uh, the meaning of the words you didn't know?

CAROLE: Well, you try and figure it out by looking at the words around it. Or, uh . . . yeah, by trying to find the context that the word is used in.

HARVEY: Do you ever ask anybody else the word—what a word means? I did, I think, last week, I asked once. It's been a long time since I asked anybody. How about you?

CAROLE: Yeah, sure. I often ask people—if they're around.

Speaking Activities—Words in Context

I

Answer on the basis of the Listening Text:

Is it possible to find out the meaning of a word without looking it up in the dictionary?

Is it sometimes easy to guess the meaning of a word from its context? Why?

Imagine a person has run across a word he doesn't know. What would you tell him to do?

II

Give some suggestions for learning new words, based on your own experience.

III

Discuss the advantages and disadvantages of using a dictionary to get information about new words.

IV

Talk about the possible setting and speakers for each of the following six short conversations.

1. A. Did you hear about Fancy Nancy, the actress?
   B. Yeah, she got married for the eleventh time yesterday. She must be quite a girl.
2. A. I hear Joe has a new girl.
   B. Yeah, he sure dropped the other one fast.
3. A. What's the matter? You look sort of funny today.
   B. Oh, I forgot and left my glasses at home.
4. A. Look! These essays are almost word-for-word the same.
   B. Something funny's going on here.
5. A. Will you ask the boy for more coffee, please?
   B. Waiter! Coffee, please.
6. A. What time do you suppose the boys'll get home, Margaret?
   B. I havent the slightest idea, Annie. You know those poker games
      . . .

V

Can you answer the questions which follow each story below by using context clues in the stories?

First Story: A car. SLAM!
Mrs. Monroe ran to the front door, floury hands patting apron, collar, hair. "Albert! You're home!"
Flour flew as her arms clasped his neck. She hung there sobbing. Then at arms' length, staring at him . . .
He noticed where his jacket button had left a red imprint on her right cheek.

1. Where was Mrs. Monroe when she heard the car?
2. What had she been doing?
3. What is Albert's job or occupation?
4. How old are Albert and Mrs. Monroe?
5. What relationship are they to each other?
6. How long had Albert been away?

Second Story: Janet watched the others coming into the classroom. When Don came in, she took her books off the desk beside her and put them on the floor under her seat, Don slumped down next to her, breathing heavily, and said. "My legs are killing me! If they have many more power failures in this building, either I'll have to reduce, or they'll have to move this class downstairs!"

1. Did Janet know Don very well?

2. What had Don done just before coming into the classroom?

3. How does Don usually get to the classroom?

4. Where is the classroom?

5. What can you guess about Don's eating habits?

VI

Make up a story of your own like those in V. Tell it to your classmates and see if they can guess the situation from the context clues.

Vocabulary Study—Words in Context

I. *look at, look for, look up*

Fill in each blank in the sentences below with *at, for,* or *up,* according to which one gives the most sensible meaning to the sentence.

1. Is it always necessary to look _____ unknown words in a dictionary?

2. Look _____ each sentence and decide what goes in the blank.

3. Have you looked _____ a word in the dictionary today?

4. He looked _____ the word in his small dictionary but he couldn't find it.

5. Look _____ this word: *unfamiliar*. What are its two parts?

6. He couldn't find a synonym for *fission* although he looked _____ one.

7. He looked _____ context clues in surrounding sentences.

8. Sometimes you can look right _____ a context clue without noticing it.

9. He looked _____ his dictionary but he couldn't find it anywhere.

10. Do you remember the definitions of all the words that you look _____?

II. Notice that the adjectives in the left column can be made negative by prefixing *un-* and the adjectives in the right column can be made negative by prefixing *in-* (*im-* before *p*).

un-	available	*in-/im-*	appropriate
	familiar		correct
	known		practical

Fill in the blanks below with the negative forms of these adjectives. Use each adjective only once.

When you run across an (1)_____ or (2)_____ word, a dictionary might be (3)_____, or even if it is available, it might sometimes be (4)_____ to use. Even when you use a dictionary, you must be careful not to choose a definition (5)_____ to the context of the word that you are looking up. That is, you must pay attention to context if you don't want to select an (6)_____ meaning.

III. The following words and phrases are from the Reading Text in the paragraphs indicated. Find the word or phrase in the Listening Text paragraphs which are nearest in meaning to each of these words and phrases and write them in the blanks. (R-1 = Reading Text, paragraph 1; L-1 = Listening Text, paragraph 1, and so forth).

1. (R-1) encounter   (L-1) _____
2. (R-2) context   (L-2) _____
3. (R-2) unlock the meaning of (L-2) _____
4. (R-3) chain of thought   (L-2) _____
5. (R-5) thought   (L-6) _____

Answers to Vocabulary Study—Words in Context

I. 1. up
    2. at
    3. up
    4. for
    5. at
    6. for
    7. for
    8. at
    9. for
    10. up

II. 1. unfamiliar OR unknown
    2. unfamiliar OR unknown
    3. unavailable
    4. impractical
    5. inappropriate
    6. incorrect

III. 1. run across
    2. setting
    3. figure out the meaning of
    4. train of thought
    5. figured

Forms of Address

Discuss these key terms:

forms of address
title
first name
last name
status

Listen to or read the summary below. Then try to answer the questions that follow:

SUMMARY

In American English people call each other either by first name or by a title like Mr. or Mrs. plus last name. These are forms of address, and the form of address that a person uses reflects his relationship with the person that he is talking to. There are three possible patterns. The first is for both speakers to use first names, the second is for both to use titles plus last names, and the third is for one to say first name to the other and to receive title plus last name from him. Two people did some research on what makes people choose to use the forms of address that they do. They found out that the form a person uses depends on the age and the status of the person that he is speaking to in relation to his own age and status.

QUESTIONS

1. What are the two ways that people usually address each other in American English?
2. What are the three possible patterns of address?
3. Does the age of the person you are speaking to have anything to do with the form of address that you use?

4. Does the status of the person you are speaking to have anything to
   do with the form of address that you use?

For suggested directions for doing these lessons see page 2 of this book.

Reading Text—Forms of Address*

   (1) When one speaker speaks to another, he usually calls the person
that he is speaking to either by his first name or by a title plus his last name.
The title is ordinarily *Mr., Miss,* or *Mrs.* The first name can be referred to
as FN and the title plus the last name as TLN. *Richard* is an example of
an FN and *Mr. Gregory* is an example of a TLN. The form of address that
a speaker uses at any particular time depends on the relationship between
him and the person that he is speaking to. Three patterns are possible. Both
speakers may use FN, both may use TLN, or one may use FN and the
other TLN.

   (2) Roger Brown and Marguerite Ford have done some research on the
ways that people in the United States use these forms of address. They
gathered the data upon which they based their conclusions from two kinds
of sources: (1) American plays performed since 1939, and (2) observations
of real-life usage made by men in business firms. Their conclusions are
summarized below.

   (3) Most commonly in the United States both speakers use FN. The use
of TLN by both speakers is usually found only between adults who have
just been introduced. Newly introduced adults usually start out calling each
other by TLN, but very quickly both shift to FN, though it takes a little
longer with older than with younger people and a little longer with people
of the opposite sex than with people of the same sex. The degree of intimacy
does not have to be very great for both to use FN.

   (4) In cases where one speaker uses FN and the other TLN, there are
usually differences in age or in occupational status. Children say TLN to
adults and receive FN. Among adults, one who is the older by about 15 or
more years receives TLN and gives FN to his junior. If one speaker has
higher status than the other, he says FN and receives TLN. In cases where
the older person has the humbler occupation, priority is given to occupational status. For example, a young business executive would use FN with an
elderly janitor and receive TLN.

   (5) In cases where two people start out with one using FN and the
other TLN and eventually end up using FN with each other, it is usually
the one who uses the FN who suggests to the other that they both use FN.

---

*Based on Roger W. Brown and Marguerite Ford, "Address in American English"
in *Language in Culture and Society*, edited by Dell Hymes, New York, Harper and
Row, Publishers, 1964, pp. 234–44.

If the one who has been using TLN starts using FN without some kind of encouragement from the other, the other might consider him forward and disrespectful. Sometimes it is difficult for a person to start using FN with someone he has been calling TLN, even when he is encouraged to do so. In such a situation, he may avoid calling the person anything at all until the period of awkwardness has passed.

Listening Text—Forms of Address

(1) In American English, the most common ways of addressing a person that you're speaking to are by his first name or by a title like Mr. or Mrs. or Miss plus the last name. *Richard* is an example of a first name and *Mr. Peterson* is an example of a title plus a last name. When two people are speaking, there are three possible combinations. They use first names with each other, or they may use title plus last name with each other, or one may say first name and receive title plus last name.

(2) Roger Brown and Marguerite Ford have tried to find out what determines the way people address each other. That is, they have tried to find out under what circumstances people use first names and under what circumstances they use title plus last names.

(3) They looked for examples in a number of modern American plays, and also they asked people in business firms to report on the different forms of address that they heard in those firms.

(4) They found that the most common form of address in the United States was for both speakers to use first names. Generally, only adults who have just met call each other by *Mr.* or *Mrs.* or *Miss*, and it doesn't take them long to move to a first-name basis. People don't have to know each other very well at all to start using first names with each other.

(5) In the case where a person says *Mr.* or *Mrs.* or *Miss* to someone who calls him by his first name, he is usually the younger or else he has the lower status of the two speakers. For example, a child will call an adult *Mr. So-and-so*, but an adult will call a child *Bill* or *Mary*, or *Susie* or *Henry*, or whatever the child's name happens to be. With adults, if one adult is younger than the other by about 15 or more years, he says title plus last name and receives first name. If it happens that the older person has lower status, then he says title plus last name to the younger person and receives first name. For example, a young business executive named *Mr. Hogan* might call an elderly janitor *Henry,* if that was his first name. Henry would call the young executive *Mr. Hogan*. In other words, if age and status come into conflict, status wins out.

(6) In these unequal combinations, it may be that sometimes there is a shift to first-name basis for both. But it's usually the one who is already saying first name who takes the initiative, and it might take a while for

the other to get used to saying first name to a person he's never called by first name before. If the one who has been saying title plus last name and receiving first name starts to use first name with the other without any encouragement, the other might think he's disrespectful.

Discussion—Forms of Address

NOTES AND QUESTIONS ON DISCUSSION TAPE AND TEXT

In this conversation the woman is from Hawaii and the man is from the Midwest.

Some questions to explore:

How does the woman show that she is listening?

What is the approximate age of the speakers (teen-agers, young adults, middle-aged or elderly persons)?

Is this the beginning of the conversation?

Do you think that the speakers are good friends?

What do you think the marital status of the speakers is?

Study help:

"kind of touchy" refers to a situation in which someone may be easily offended

DISCUSSION

HARVEY: What about if you're introduced to a friend's wife, for instance. What would you do?

KATHY: Ah, well, if I call that friend by first name, and then meet his wife, I'll probably start out calling his wife by "Mrs."

HARVEY: Even though you call him by the first name?

KATHY: Yeah, because—I don't know—that's really kind of touchy there.

HARVEY: Yeah, well for me especially as a man, it's even worse. I, I don't think I ever start calling any—anybody's wife by the first name. You know, never right at the beginning, when I'm introduced, even though I'm calling—the husband's a real good friend. I don't think I ever—Well, usually I avoid using the name.

KATHY: Yes.

HARVEY: I may say "Hi" or "Hello" but I think I avoid calling them you know—just because it's sort of an awkward situation, I don't even bother.

KATHY: Uh-huh. I'm not sure it's more of a problem for you or me—it's the "other woman" kind of thing.

HARVEY: Oh, yeah, yeah—especially if you know him well.

KATHY: But usually when it's somebody's wife—you'll be introduced to them—where he'll use her, his, her first name. And uh he doesn't say, "This is Aileen Somebody, my wife—he'll say—just say, "Aileen."

HARVEY: Yeah.

KATHY: But, still, I'll say, "Mrs. Somebody."

HARVEY: Yeah, yeah. Well, you're sort of in a spot, in that situation.

KATHY: Mm, hmm.

Speaking Activities—Forms of Address

I

Answer on the basis of the Listening Text:

What did Roger Brown and Marguerite Ford notice about adults who have just met each other?

If one person uses a title and the other uses the first name when they talk together, what might this imply about their relationship?

Is it easy to move to first name basis with someone? When is it easy and when is it difficult?

Did anything in this text surprise you?

II

How many English forms of address can you think of? When are they used?

III

Do you know a person that you address in different ways at different times? Discuss.

IV

"What's in a name?" Shakespeare once wrote. If you had to answer the question "What's in a title?" what would you say? Give examples from your language.

V

In English "I" can always be used by a speaker to refer to himself. Is that true in your language? Discuss.

VI

If an older woman is introduced to you as Mary Smith, what might you do to find out how she would prefer you to address her?

Vocabulary Study—Forms of Address

I. The following items are taken from the Reading Text. In the Listening Text there are items which correspond to them. Find these items in the Listening Text and write them in the blanks.

Example: (R-1) Three patterns are possible.

(L-1) *There are three possible patterns.*

NOTE: R-1 = Reading Text, paragraph 1, etc.; L-1 = Listening Text, paragraph 1, and so forth.

1. (R-3) Newly introduced adults. . . .
   (L-4) _____

2. (R-3) very quickly both shift to FN
   (L-4) _____

3. (R-3) The degree of intimacy does not have to be very great.
   (L-4) _____

4. (R-4) humbler occupation
   (L-5) _____

5. (R-5) . . . the other might consider him forward and disrespectful.
   (L-6) _____

II. Copy the sentences below, replacing the italicized item with the item of similar meaning from the following list. You can find the answer by looking at the sentences in the Reading and Listening Texts.

looked for	call
depends on	is found
gathered	move

1. (R-2) They *collected* the data from two sources.

   _____

2. (L-4) It doesn't take them long to *shift* to a first-name basis.

   _____

3. (L-5) A young business executive might *address* an elderly janitor by his first name.

_____

4. (R-1) The form of address that a speaker uses *is a function of* the relationship between him and the person that he is speaking to.

_____

_____

5. (R-3) The use of TLN by both speakers usually *occurs* only between adults who have just been introduced.

_____

_____

6. (L-3) They *searched for* examples in a number of modern American plays.

_____

III. Each of the sentences below contains a form of *gather*. Above each occurrence of *gather* write a synonym from the following list:

get the idea
collect
come together
pick

1. I *gather* that you don't like him.
2. He *gathered* from what she said that she was annoyed.
3. Before the hike, the leaders *gathered* the hikers *together* for instructions.
4. She *gathered* the kittens *up* and put them in the basket.
5. They often *gather* at Mr. Hubert's house to listen to his records.
6. They *gathered* on the beach for a picnic.
7. I *gather* that you're going somewhere.
8. He's been *gathering* information for his paper for a month.
9. Let's *gather (together)* in about fifteen minutes.
10. He *gathered* the lettuce from his garden.
11. They went into the field and *gathered* some wild flowers.
12. Have the cherries been *gathered*?

Answers to Vocabulary Study—Forms of Address

I. 1. adults who have just met
   2. it doesn't take them long to move to a first name basis
   3. People don't have to know each other very well at all . . .

  4. lower status
  5. The other might think he's disrespectful

II. 1. gather
  2. move
  3. call
  4. depends on
  5. is found
  6. looked for

III. 1. get the idea
  2. got the idea
  3. collected
  4. collected
  5. come together, collect
  6. came together, collected
  7. get the idea
  8. collecting
  9. come together, collect
  10. picked
  11. picked
  12. picked

The Environment and the Automobile

Discuss these key terms:

energy problems
energy consumption
to conserve energy
blackouts
fuel shortages
rising fuel prices

Listen to or read the summary below. Then try to answer the questions that follow:

SUMMARY

People in the United States are aware that the automobile has a great influence on many aspects of their lives, such as their social lives, the economy, and the environment. People are also aware that in the past few years there have been energy problems such as blackouts, fuel shortages, and rising fuel prices. People are not so aware, however, of the relation between the automobile and these energy problems. The fact is that in the course of a year the automobile is responsible for about 25 percent of the energy consumption in the United States. We need to turn to other means of passenger transportation in order to conserve energy.

QUESTIONS

1. What are some of the aspects of life that the automobile influences?
2. What kinds of energy problems have people been having in the past few years?

3. Is there a relation between the automobile and energy problems? What is the relation?

For suggested directions for doing these lessons see page 2 of this book.

Reading Text—The Environment and the Automobile*

(1) The automobile is assuming an ever increasing role in the social life, the economy, and the environment of America. Environmental problems associated with the automobile include air and noise pollution, traffic congestion, urban decay, suburban sprawl, and the lack of adequate transportation alternatives, such as mass transit systems.

(2) During the past few years we have also been confronted with a series of energy problems, often referred to as energy crisis: brownouts and blackouts, fuel shortages, rising fuel prices, and the environmental impacts of energy production and conversion. Unfortunately, many of us are not aware of the close relationship between the automobile and these energy issues.

(3) Approximately one-half of the United States energy consumption is supplied by petroleum, with half of this petroleum going to the transportation sector. In 1970, American cars consumed 66 billion gallons of gasoline, equal to 30 percent of total United States petroleum consumption. . . .

(4) But gasoline consumption by automobiles is only part of the problem. Indirectly, to manufacture, sell, and maintain it, the automobile consumes as much energy as it consumes directly in gasoline. . . .

(5) All together, to manufacture one automobile it takes about 150 Btu. (British thermal units) of energy, which is the equivalent of 1,100 gallons of gasoline. This is enough gasoline to run a car for about 15,000 miles.

(6) Energy is also required to ship cars from the factories to dealerships throughout the country. Dealers expend energy preparing cars for delivery, advertising their wares, lighting and heating their showrooms, and so on. These various activities require almost as much energy per automobile as does the manufacture of a car. We must also include the energy used to make replacement tires, spark plugs, batteries, and all other parts needed for repairs and maintenance and as accessories.

(7) Once the automobile reaches the consumer, it must be powered. In order to produce a gallon of gasoline, oil fields must be discovered, wells drilled, oil pumped to the surface and transported to refineries. Petroleum

*From Eric Hirst, "In Praise of Bikers, Hikers, and Crowded Cars," reprinted from *Natural History* Magazine, August-September, 1972. Copyright © The American Museum of Natural History 1972. Reprinted by permission.

refineries consume energy to transform crude oil into various refined petroleum products, such as gasoline, diesel fuel, kerosine, and jet fuel. Totaling the energy costs for these steps suggests that about 1.2 units of energy are required, directly or indirectly, to produce 1 unit of gasoline energy. In other words, the energy equivalent of 12 gallons is consumed for every 10 gallons pumped into your car's gas tank.

(8) Finally, billions of dollars are spent annually to construct new highways and roads. This requires considerable quantities of energy, both for the construction itself and for the production of the sand, gravel, and cement used to build these roads.

(9) In 1968, for example, all these energy requirements added up to a total of about 16,000 trillion Btu. Of this total, only 50 percent was consumed directly as gasoline; the remainder was devoted to indirect functions. The average automobile in the United States consumes 19,000 Btu. per mile. This is equivalent to only 7.1 miles per gallon of gasoline.

(10) Thus, the automobile is responsible, directly and indirectly, for about 25 percent of the total United States energy consumption. What can we do to lower this figure, conserve energy resources, reduce air pollution, and help solve both our energy and automobile problems? The most important thing is to promote changes in passenger transportation. Bicycles are 22 times as energy-efficient as cars, walking 18 times, buses almost 4 times, and railroads 2.5 times. Only airplanes are less energy-efficient than cars.

(11) . . . In addition to the beneficial aspects of energy conservation, such changes in transportation would have other positive effects. Traffic congestion in cities would be reduced, and land formerly devoted to parking lots and streets could be used for parks and housing. The noise of engines, squealing tires, and honking horns would be gone and we might, once again, be able to hear birds sing.

(12) . . . Unfortunately, it will take at least a few decades to shift from automobiles to more energy-efficient transport modes such as mass transit. One encouraging note, however: in 1971 more than 8 million bicycles were sold, twice the number sold ten years earlier.

(13) In the meantime, there are ways to increase the energy-efficiency of cars. The typical car carries only two passengers: if this number were increased to four, energy consumption for automobiles would be halved. We could also use smaller cars, with low-horsepower engines, driven at lower speeds to improve fuel economy. . . .

(14) Some of these gains, however, will be offset by a probable decline of 20 to 40 percent in fuel economy over the next several years; to meet the new federal automotive air quality requirements, car engines will use more gasoline to clean up their exhaust.

(15) The changes in passenger transportation suggested here would require modifications of many elements of our society. But this should not deter us from considering such changes. After all, consider the alternatives.

Listening Text—The Environment and the Automobile

(1) People in the United States are becoming more and more aware of the influence of the automobile on their lives. The automobile has an influence on social life, on the economy, and on the environment. It is particularly its influence on the environment that people are increasingly worrying about. It has become obvious that the automobile contributes to air and noise pollution, traffic congestion, urban decay, and suburban sprawl, and that it has kept mass transit systems from developing.

(2) People are not so aware, however, of the relation between the automobile and energy problems. In the past few years the country has had energy problems such as brownouts and blackouts, fuel shortages, rising fuel prices, and bad effects on the environment caused by producing energy and converting it from one form to another.

(3) These energy problems are in fact closely related to the automobile. An enormous amount of energy, supplied mainly by petroleum, is required by the automobile. In fact, the automobile is responsible for 25 percent of the total energy consumption in the United States.

(4) Gasoline is only part of the energy required. It also takes energy to manufacture the automobile in the first place. Then it must be transported to dealers who advertise and sell it, all of which takes energy. Energy is also required to make replacement parts for automobile repair. Once the cars is on the road, energy still must go into producing gasoline for it. Oil fields must be discovered. Oil must be pumped to the surface and refined. And think of the energy required annually to build and maintain highways and roads.

(5) All together the energy requirements of a car are about 50 percent for gasoline and 50 percent for all these other needs that we have just mentioned. The question is, what can we do about all this? What can we do to lower this figure, to conserve energy resources so as to reduce air pollution and help solve both our energy and automobile problems?

(6) The most important thing we can do is to promote changes in passenger transportation. Bicycles are 22 times as energy-efficient as cars, walking 18 times, buses almost 4 times, and railroads 2.5 times. Only airplanes are less energy-efficient than cars. If we promote such changes, we won't only conserve energy. We will also reduce the crowding and noise in the cities and we can use land for parks instead of for parking lots.

(7) It will take time for such changes to come about. Fortunately the sale of bicycles is increasing. And one thing we can do immediately is to increase the energy-efficiency of cars by using smaller cars and carrying more passengers.

(8) These changes that have just been suggested will require other changes in our society too, which some people may resist. It will not be easy to make these changes. But consider the alternatives.

Discussion—The Environment and the Automobile

NOTES ON THE DISCUSSION TOPIC AND TEXT

This discussion is an informal discussion between two men. The subject is based on the last point of the Reading Text. One of the men is from the Midwest and the other is from the South.

Some questions to explore:

How well do these men know each other?

Is this a formal or an informal conversation?

Where do you think the conversation takes place?

Are the speakers equal in status?

DISCUSSION

LARRY: I don't know, either, what, uh . . . in his, uh, final statement he says "Consider the alternatives" and, quite frankly, I don't think the alternatives are so bad that we're going to do anything within the next few years.

HARVEY: You mean, uh (Larry: if we don't) we're going to do something, we're going to do something about the pollution but we aren't going to do anything about the high energy consumption?

LARRY: No. Right. But we're (Harvey: Yeah, yeah) something's being done about the pollution problem, and it's, it's the talk of the town now (Harvey: Sure, sure) At least it's, that's in vogue, but as far as, for—What he's dealing with here, which is the major problem, (Harvey: Right, it's the energy consumption) it seems to me, we're not aware of that.

HARVEY: No, no this's new to me (Larry: The problem, the problem is not, huh?) I didn't even think about it before. I might've, I think it dimly—I'd run across it some place—that he, the energy, uh, required to make a car, but it, it never struck me as (Larry: as being all that important) being all that much, yeah.

LARRY: And life or death that he talks about, as you know, it's like it is life or death when he says "consider the alternatives."

Speaking Activities—The Environment and the Automobile

I

Answer on the basis of the Listening Text:

What are people in the U.S. becoming aware of?
What are some of the facts that the author mentions about the auto-
   mobile?
What should people consider doing in place of driving cars?
What are some of the changes that people will resist making?

II

Do you come to class by car? Why?

III

Discuss the different kinds of pollution—air, water, noise, visual, and
so on—and their causes.

IV

What are the alternatives referred to in the last paragraph of the
Reading and Listening Texts? Discuss.

V

What are some of the reasons that it is so difficult to get man to stop
polluting his environment?

VI

Does your country have pollution problems? Energy depletion problems? Discuss.

Vocabulary Study—The Environment and the Automobile

I. Each of the four sentences below contains an underlined word
   which refers to a span of time. The first two sentences are from the
   reading selection; the second two are not.

1. Billions of dollars are spent <u>annually</u> to construct new highways and roads. (R-8)
2. It will take at least a few <u>decades</u> to shift from automobiles to more energy-efficient transport modes.
3. People are concerned about keeping the world habitable for future <u>generations</u>.
4. It took many <u>aeons</u> for petroleum to develop in the earth.

What length of time does each of these words refer to?

annually _____

decade _____

generation _____

aeon _____

II. The words in the left column are nouns and those in the right column are verbs which are related to those nouns. The underlined words are those which appear in the Reading Text in the paragraphs indicated.

Fill the blanks in the sentences below with the appropriate words. The first one is done as an example.

R-1	<u>pollution</u>		pollute
R-2	<u>conversion</u>		convert
R-3	<u>consumption</u>	R-4	<u>consume</u>
R-8	<u>construction</u>	R-8	<u>construct</u>
R-11	<u>conservation</u>		conserve
R-15	<u>modification</u>		modify

1. Automobile fumes _*pollute*_ the air.
   Automobile fumes contribute to air _*pollution*_ .
2. One way to _____ energy is to walk or ride a bicycle instead of driving a car.
   Energy _____ will allow us to use land for housing instead of highways.
3. The _____ of many elements in our society will be necessary before we can make changes in passenger transportation.
   It is not easy for people to _____ their ways.
4. Gasoline _____ by an automobile accounts for only part of the energy that it _____.
5. Lots of money is spent each year to _____ highways.
   The _____ of highways requires much expenditure of energy.
6. Crude oil is _____ into refined petroleum products, such as gasoline. This _____ of energy from one form to another has an impact on the environment.

III. Match the meanings on the right with the words on the left by placing the letters in the appropriate parentheses. All the words are from the first paragraph of the listening text.

(   ) congestion   a. city
(   ) sprawl   b. a crowded condition
(   ) decay   c. wearing out and falling apart
(   ) urban   d. outside the city
(   ) suburban   e. spread out over a large area

IV. In the following sentences some counting verbs are underlined. Indicate the number each verb is related to by writing the number (or the fraction) in the blank in front of the sentence.

_____ 1. If you halve four, you get two.
_____ 2. if you double four, you get eight.
_____ 3. If you triple four, you get twelve.
_____ 4. If you quadruple four, you get sixteen.

Answers to Vocabulary Study— The Environment and the Automobile

I. 1. one year
   2. ten years
   3. about 25 years
   4. an immeasurably long time

II. 1. pollute, pollution
   2. conserve, conservation
   3. modification, modify
   4. consumption, consumes
   5. construct, construction
   6. converted, conversion

III. b
   e
   c
   a
   d

IV. 1. 1/2
   2. 2
   3. 3
   4. 4

Food for Thought

Discuss these key terms:

accumulate
food for thought
fallacies
fads
myths
religious restrictions
social status

Listen to or read the summary below. Then try to answer the questions that follow.

SUMMARY

One could tell many interesting stories about foods. Many myths, fallacies, and fads about them have accumulated over the centuries. The effects of certain foods on those who eat them, religious restrictions on the use of certain foods, and the effect of social status on one's eating habits are some of the things which provide food for thought.

QUESTIONS

1. What kind of stories can be told about food?
2. What are some of the things which provide food for thought?
3. How long have stories about food existed?

For suggested directions for doing these lessons see page 2 of this book.

Reading Text—Food for Thought*

(1) Myths, fallacies and fads have been built up over centuries. They change a bit but they are hardy and keep coming back in a slightly different form. From the medicine man to the present food faddist, it has been a profitable business to exploit them. But many people sincerely believe them.

(2) The primitive hunter believed that his courage would be increased if he ate the heart of a hero or a lion. This is one myth that most of us can laugh about, but don't be too sure someone doesn't still believe this.

(3) The belief that fish is brain food may have originated in some area where protein foods were scarce except for fish. It may well have been that those pregnant women and infants who ate fish were more intelligent than those who ate exclusively vegetables, fruits and grains.

(4) A relatively new fact resulting from research has shown that the number of brain cells is smaller when the protein eaten by the mother and the baby is lower than it should be. In that case, fish was a brain food, but so are all sources of protein.

(5) Many religions use food for symbolism as in the bread and wine of communion or in the restriction of certain foods on special occasions such as the use of meats on fast days by the Catholic Church or the use of pork by the Jews and Mohammedans. The rules for slaughtering animals by the Jews and the Mohammedans are another example. And to a Hindu, a cow is a sacred animal protected from slaughter and from use as food.

(6) Other foods are forbidden to Hindus and the most pious are strict vegetarians who do not even eat eggs. Many young people today are turning to Hinduism and Buddhism and adopting the food restrictions of those religions.

(7) Class and wealth determine food habits also. In many cultures, the lower classes were forbidden to eat some foods. These were usually reserved for the higher castes.

(8) The use of white rice in many Asian countries was limited to the wealthy because they could afford the cost of milling. This constituted status. When people came to Hawaii they found that white rice was available to everyone, but they still felt that they had reached a higher status even though the white rice was lower in nutritional value than the whole grain rice.

(9) Food gives emotional satisfaction in many ways. Some people eat because they are frustrated and unhappy. The reducing diets which promise that you can eat your weight off appeal to this kind of person. Milk is tied

*Marjorie Abel, "Food Fads and Myths Are Nothing New." *Honolulu Star-Bulletin*, Section D-11, Wednesday, November 19, 1969. Reprinted with permission.

to memories of home and mother so people away from home drink more milk.

(10) The scare technique of telling people that their food is poisoned by sprays or chemical fertilizers, or does not have adequate nutritive value because it is grown on worn out soil, seems to be modern. These people claim that organic fertilizer is the only way to grow high value foods.

(11) Actually, if soil is worn out, the nutritive value of a pound of food grown on it is the same as that grown on soil fertilized either organically or inorganically. There simply will be more pounds growing on the fertilized field. The highest yield of all is reported by some as coming from soil which is fertilized both ways.

Listening Text—Food for Thought

(1) Many untrue stories about foods have built up over the years and many people believe these stories. Primitive hunters thought their courage would increase if they ate the heart of a lion. Some people today believe that the eating of fish increases one's intelligence. This may be so, but only insofar as fish is a source of protein, which does affect the growth of the brain.

(2) Food symbolism is used in many religions; for example, the bread and wine of communion in Christian churches and the restrictions on the use of various foods in other religions. Very pious Hindus are strict vegetarians.

(3) Sometimes a person's social status can determine his food habits. Only the wealthy ate white rice in many Asian countries. In Hawaii people found white rice available to all. It was lower in nutritional value than whole grain rice but they continued using it because it still indicated a higher social status.

(4) Food can give emotional satisfaction. This is why some people eat a lot when they are unhappy. Some people drink more milk when they are away from home because milk is tied to memories of home and mother. The nutritive value of food is not affected by the fertility of the soil. The people who say that the use of organic fertilizer is the only way to grow high value food are wrong.

Discussion—Food for Thought

NOTES AND QUESTIONS ON DISCUSSION TAPE AND TEXT

In this discussion, one of the speakers is from New Jersey and the other one is from Arkansas.

Some questions to explore:

What has gone on before this discussion?
It this a formal or informal situation?
What is the relationship between the speakers?
Why does Dr. Recchi use "we" in his response to the questions?

DISCUSSION

DR. RECCHI: Are there any questions? Mr. Smith.

MR. SMITH: Yes, sir. You spoke basically of—uh—three areas connected with food. The effect that people believe they may get by eating certain food, religious restrictions, and then—uh—

DR. RECCHI: Uh—er—could I interrupt you just a minute please. Would you repeat the first part of your question?

MR. SMITH: You spoke of three—basically three areas connected with food. The first, how people believe certain foods provide different things, for instance, eating the lion's heart was supposed to provide hunters with courage; then you spoke of—uh—religious restrictions and symbolism and—uh—you spoke of social status—the white rice in Hawaii, for instance. Now, can you tell me which of these do you feel is most important? Is one of these areas more important than the others?

DR. RECCHI: Well, I—I'm not so sure we can speak in terms of importance in this case, since—uh—our lecture was concerned mainly with—uh—stories and anecdotes—uh—we spoke of myths and fallacies and fads that have built up over the years about foods and uh— they're really more a matter of interest rather than importance. Wouldn't you say so?

MR. SMITH: Yes, I—I suppose so. Now, in this line of thinking, let me—uh—question you concerning the milk incident. Uh—the—what seems to me rather ridiculous, that when one is away from home he drinks more milk because it reminds him of home and mother.

DR. RECCHI: Uh—I didn't make up the story. It was told to me by someone else; however—uh—I've—uh—seen some things which might tend to verify it. I've notice that—uh—students from Asia who come to Hawaii often drink much more milk here than they would in their own country. Uh—now this may be due to the fact that—the— milk is unavailable where they come from. On the other hand, it may also be due to this—uh—uh—psychological phenomenon that's —uh—mentioned in the story that we told.

Speaking Activities—Food for Thought

I

Answer on the basis of the Listening Text:

What do you think primitive hunters believed about lions?
What does the author mention about Hindus?
How is what people eat sometimes determined?
What do you think about food fads?

II

How do your eating habits change when you are away from home?

III

What food restrictions are common in your country? Do you know what these restrictions are based on?

IV

Are you familiar with any special occasions that have special foods associated with them? Discuss.

V

In your opinion, what foods have high social status? Which have low social status?

VI

Are there any things which people should not eat? Discuss.

Vocabulary Study—Food for Thought

I. Change each item below into a compound noun. All the answers can be found in the Reading Text in the paragraphs indicated

(R-1 = Reading Text, paragraph 1, and so forth). The first one is done as an example.

NOTE: In a compound noun, the first element receives more stress than the second element. Some compound nouns are written as one word and some as two words.

1. man who practices medicine (in a primitive way)
   (R-1) *medicine man*

2. person who follows fads in food
   (R-1) _____

3. food for the brain
   (R-3) _____

4. cells in the brain
   (R-4) _____

5. days when one fasts
   (R-5) _____

6. restrictions on food
   (R-6) _____

7. rice which is white (milled)
   (R-8) _____

8. rice which is whole grain
   (R-8) _____

9. diets for reducing
   (R-9) _____

10. technique for scaring
    (R-10) _____

II. When the words *bread* and *wine* are used together, they are used in that order rather than in the reverse order, *wine* and *bread*. Below are some pairs of words. Join them using either *and* or *or*, as you think appropriate. Put them in the order that you think they commonly occur in. The first one is done as an example.

1. bread
   wine _*bread and wine*_

2. eggs
   ham _____

3. home
   house _____

4. laugh
   cry _____

5. true
   false _____

6. wrong
   right _____

7. on
   off _____

8. rich
   poor _____

9. fowl
   fish _____

10. women
    children _____

Answers to Vocabulary Study—Food for Thought

I. 1. medicine man

    2. food faddist

    3. brain food

    4. brain cells

    5. fast days

    6. food restrictions

    7. white rice

    8. whole grain rice

    9. reducing diets

   10. scare technique

NOTE: Notice that all these compound words are written as two words. Examples of compound nouns written as one word are *housewife, blackboard, wastebasket.*

II. 1. bread and wine

    2. ham and eggs

    3. house and home

    4. laugh or cry, laugh and cry

    5. true or false, true and false

    6. right or wrong, right and wrong

    7. off and on

    8. rich or poor, rich and poor

    9. fish or fowl, fish and fowl

   10. women and children

Part II

DEVELOPING COMPETENCE IN ENGLISH

What does it mean to "learn" the rules of grammar that we apply so carefully when we first speak a foreign language? It does *not* mean to memorize the formulations of the rules from a grammar book. Let us take again the example of chess: the most efficient way to master the rules of chess would not be to memorize the official rule booklet. Instead one should have a teacher who would show him how to move each piece, and how to castle, and how to capture the opponent's pieces. The teacher would help him make the moves and would guide him through his first game. Rules for action are best learned in conjunction with demonstration and practice of the action. The particular formulation of the rules is not terribly important: the rules of chess could probably be explained by sign language alone. But suppose instead of explaining the rules you had a learner memorize some championship games: how much longer would it take for a person to figure out the simple moves that each piece can make! So it is with language. A few carefully chosen examples of a rule in operation can lead us to understand the rule. But embedding these examples in a dialog to be memorized might mask their significance entirely.

> Karl Conrad Diller, *Generative Grammar,*
> *Structural Linguistics, and Language*
> *Teaching* (Rowley, Mass.: Newbury House
> Publishers, 1971), pp. 26–27.

Viewing language learning as the internalization of rules rather than the formation of habits suggests that classroom grammar exercises should also be viewed differently. Instead of being the means for instilling habits, these exercises can now be conceived of as one means of allowing the students to react to and manipulate data in order to internalize rules. Thus, the student no longer acquires a set of overt habits. Instead, he acquires a set of internal rules which allow him to use the language creatively, producing and understanding sentences he has never heard before.

> Robert Krohn, "The Role of Linguistics
> in TEFL Methodology," *Language Learning*,
> XX, No. 1 (June 1970), 105.

Directions

There are nine sentence study lessons in Part II. Each sentence study lesson corresponds to the lesson of the same number in Part I. A sentence study lesson should be done after the corresponding lesson in Part I has been completed, since all the sentences in each sentence study lesson are about the topic of that lesson. For example, Lesson 1 in Part I is on proverbs, and all the sentences in Sentence Study 1 in Part II are on proverbs; Lesson 2 in Part I is on folk medicine, and all the sentences in Sentence Study 2 in Part II are on folk medicine, and so on.

The main purpose of the sentence study lessons is to give you practice in combining sentences by turning one sentence into a noun-expression and inserting it into a noun slot in the other sentence. The process of turning a sentence into a noun-expression which can then be used as the subject, object, or complement in another sentence is called nominalization.

These nine sentence study lessons are designed for you to work through at your own speed. The directions for doing the lessons are as follows:

Each lesson has from four to six parts, numbered I, II, III, and so on. Sometimes one of these parts has three subdivisions—A, B, and C.

If a part has no subdivisions, you should do the whole part.

If a part has three subdivisions, this is the procedure you are to follow:

1. Read the directions for A and do the first few items in A.
2. If you think that A is too easy for you, do not complete it. Do B, and then do C.
3. If you have any trouble doing B, you had better go back and complete A.

The answers are at the end of each sentence study lesson, so that you can correct your own work.

Glossary of Grammatical Terms

Here are some terms that you will find used in the Sentence Study Lessons:

active sentence An active sentence has a verb in the active voice. For example: *He wrote a letter.*

complement A complement is the part of a sentence that completes another part of the sentence. Most often it completes the verb. A complement cannot become the subject of a passive sentence in the same way that an object can. The underlined portions of the following sentences are complements: *You can't force a person* to take medicine. *He expects* to go to the party. *He promised* that he would explain cultural variations in eye contact.

object   An object comes after a verb. Sentences with objects after their main verbs can usually be passivized. When such sentences are passivized, the object becomes the subject. The underlined portions of the following sentences are objects: *Holt mentioned* the fact that they don't experiment. *Holt mentioned* their not experimenting. The passive forms of these sentences are: *The fact that they don't experiment was mentioned* and *Their not experimenting was mentioned.*

paraphrase   A paraphrase is a rewording, that is, it is another way of saying something. For example: *The letter was written by him* is a paraphrase of *He wrote the letter.*

passive sentence   A passive sentence has a verb in the passive voice. For example: *The letter was written by him.*

split sentence   A split sentence is a sentence like *What he wrote was his name,* where *He wrote his name* has been split by putting *was* in between *He wrote* and *his name* and then putting *What* in front of the whole sentence. Another label for split sentence is *cleft sentence.*

Proverbs

Turning Sentences into Subjects and Objects:
That, Ing and For-To

OVERVIEW

I. Turning sentences into subjects by using *that*, *ing*, and *for-to*.

II. Starting sentences with *it*.

III. Turning sentences into objects by using *that* and *ing*.

IV. Turning sentences into objects by using *that* and/or *to*.

V. Summary exercise.

VI. What about meaning?

I. Turning sentences into subjects by using *that, ing*, and *for-to*.

    A. Combine each pair of sentences below and underline one of the expressions in parentheses (according to your own choice), as in the example.

               (the fact)that

Example: ⋏ Almost every language has its share of proverbs. T̶H̶I̶S̶ (surprises) (<u>doesn't surprise</u>) me.

               NOTE: The parentheses around *the fact* means that you can either put *the fact* in or leave it out.

Do not copy the sentences. Just delete and add, as in the example.

    1. Wise sayings in different languages sometimes have the same

       meaning. THIS (strikes) (doesn't strike) me as interesting.

83

2. Milner found proverbs to be a good. guide for social life in Samoa. THIS (surprised) (didn't surprise) me.

3. Different languages have similar sayings. THIS (may) (must) indicate that there is a kind of universal wisdom.

4. Milner went to the South Pacific to compile a dictionary. THIS indicates his interest in (travel) (language).

5. Milner found a rigidly stratified culture. THIS (surprises) (doesn't surprise) me.

6. They had proverbs for every human exchange. THIS (intrigues) (doesn't intrigue) me.

7. People share certain feelings about life. THIS (implies) (denies) a universal wisdom.

8. Proverbs deal in the fundamental stuff of life. THIS (should) (should not) surprise us.

B. Provide a third way of saying the subject in each of the sentences below, as in the example.

Example:

THAT   (The fact) that almost every language has its share of proverbs

ING   Almost every language having its share of proverbs

FOR-TO   *For almost every language to have its share of proverbs* doesn't surprise me.

1. THAT   (The fact) that Milner found proverbs to be a good guide for social life in Samoa

   ING   Milner's finding proverbs to be a good guide for social life in Samoa

   FOR-TO   _____

_____

didn't surprise us.

2. THAT   (The fact) that different languages have similar sayings

   ING   Different languages having similar sayings
   FOR-TO   _____

    may indicate that there as a kind of universal wisdom.

3. FOR-TO   For Milner to go to the South Pacific to compile a dictionary

   THAT   (The fact) that Milner went to the South Pacific to compile a dictionary

   ING   _____

    indicates his interest in language.

4. FOR-TO   For Milner to find a rigidly stratified culture
   THAT   (The fact) that Milner found a rigidly stratified culture

   ING   _____

    surprised some people.

5. ING   Their sharing certain feelings about life
   FOR-TO   For them to share certain feelings about life
   THAT   _____

    implies a universal wisdom.

6. FOR-TO   For them to have proverbs for every human exchange

   THAT   (The fact) that they had proverbs for every human exchange

   ING   _____

    intrigued him.

7. ING   Their dealing in the fundamental stuff of life
   FOR-TO   For them to deal in the fundamental stuff of life
   THAT   _____

    did not surprise us.

C. Answer the following questions. Base your answers on information in the Reading and Listening Texts. Answer with a THAT expression, as in the example. Do not write out complete sentences.

Example: What is one argument for proverbs having a common source?

the fact that he collected so many of them

1. What indicates Milner's belief that proverbs are significant?
   the fact that _____

2. What intrigued Milner about the Samoans?
   the fact that _____

3. What suggests that the common source of proverbs is the universality of human thought?
   the fact that _____

II. Starting sentences with *it*.

Change each of the following sentences into a sentence beginning with *it* and ending with a THAT expression, as in the example. Also underline one of the expressions in parentheses (according to the sense of the reading and listening texts).

Example: ~~The fact~~ that wise sayings in different languages sometimes have the same meaning *It* (is) (<u>is not</u>) surprising.

Do not copy the sentences. Just delete and add, as in the example.

1. The fact that they had proverbs for every human exchange (intrigued) (didn't intrigue) Milner.

2. The fact that proverbs are similar across cultures (may be) (cannot be) the result of a kind of universal wisdom.

3. That proverbs deal with the fundamental stuff of life (is) (is not) Milner's idea.

4. That proverbs in different languages share a common source is (likely) (unlikely).

5. That the universality of human thought is the source of proverbs

   is (possible) (impossible).

III. Turning sentences into objects by using *that* and *ing*.

   A. Combine each pair of sentences below, as in the example. Also underline one of the expressions in parentheses (according to the sense of the reading and listening texts).

   Example: He recalled ~~SOMETHING.~~ *(the fact) that* The Chinese have (<u>many</u>) (few) proverbs.

   NOTE: <u>*the fact*</u> is optional.

   Do not copy the sentences. Just delete and add, as in the example.

   1. He mentioned SOMETHING. Many of the sayings were (similar) (different) in meaning.

   2. He noticed SOMETHING. (The Samoans) (The Incas) used proverbs as a guide in their social life.

   3. They forgot SOMETHING. The (Americans) (Japanese) say "Too many cooks spoil the broth."

   4. He mentioned SOMETHING. (All) (Some) civilizations are rich in proverbs.

   B. Provide a second way of saying the object of the sentences below, as in the example.

   Example:
   He denied
   THAT   (the fact) that he had used that proverb.
   ING   *his having used that proverb*

   1. Did he mention
      THAT   (the fact) that the Samoans have proverbs for every human exchange?
      ING   _____
              _____

2. Do you recall

ING   his comparing proverbs from different cultures?

THAT _____

_____

3. Were you aware of

THAT   the fact that he wrote that dictionary?

ING   _____

4. He would never deny

ING   his being surprised at the similarity of proverbs across cultures.

THAT _____

C. Write four sentences. Begin each sentence with EITHER *He mentioned* or *He recalled*. End each sentence with one of the following sentences by turning it either into a THAT expression or an ING expression. The first one is done for you as an example.

Every language has its share of proverbs and wise sayings. He had heard a similar proverb in another language. The best proverbs have certain characteristics in common: They have thousands of these pithy sayings.

1. *He recalled their having thousands of these pithy sayings.*

2. _____

3. _____

4. _____

IV. Turning sentences into objects by using *that* and/or *to*. NOTE: Either *that* or *to* can be used with *believe* and *suppose*; only *that* can be used with *say, claim, maintain, mention (the fact), recall (the fact)*.

Combine each pair of sentences below, as in the examples. Use *to* wherever possible. Otherwise use *that*.

Examples: Milner believes ~~SOMETHING.~~ *to* The origin of proverbs lies in the universality of human thought.

People say ~~SOMETHING.~~ *that* Waste makes waste.

Do not copy the sentences. Just delete and add as in the example.

1. He supposes SOMETHING. Birth and death belong to the fundamental stuff of life.

2. He claims SOMETHING. People share certain feelings about life.

3. He recalled SOMETHING. The Iranians have a proverb with a
   meaning like "Too many cooks spoil the broth."

4. He maintained SOMETHING. The best proverbs transcend ethnic
   and geographic barriers.

5. He believes SOMETHING. Almost every language has its share of
   proverbs.

6. One might suppose SOMETHING. All languages have proverbs.
   But this is not so.

7. He said SOMETHING. No one knows why some people have few
   proverbs and others have many.

8. He believes SOMETHING. Proverbs offer insight into human
   thought.

9. He supposed SOMETHING. The similarity between proverbs is
   significant.

10. He mentioned SOMETHING. Proverbs say a great deal in a very
    few words.

V. Summary exercise.
   Put OK in front of each sentence that you consider correct and NO
   in front of each sentence that you consider incorrect. Correct each
   sentence that you consider incorrect. The first one is done as an
   example.

that Milner had collected OR _Milner's having collected_

_No_ 1. He recalled ~~Milner to have collected~~ thousands of
        proverbs.

_____ 2. Milner mentioned his being struck by the similarity of
        the proverbs across cultures.

_____ 3. He believes people sharing certain feelings about life.

_____ 4. That proverbs provide a clue to the common denominator of all human thought is likely.

_____ 5. He said that the Arabs minted many proverbs.

_____ 6. Milner mentioned the fact his being struck by the similarity of proverbs across cultures.

_____ 7. That some cultures produced such a meager stock of proverbs surprised him.

_____ 8. He believes that people share certain feelings about life.

_____ 9. He recalled Milner('s) having collected thousands of proverbs.

_____ 10. That proverbs providing a clue to the common denominator of all human thought is unlikely.

_____ 11. It is his idea that proverbs distill a universal wisdom.

_____ 12. He said the fact that the Arabs minted many proverbs.

_____ 13. For different languages to have similar proverbs indicates a universal wisdom.

_____ 14. Some cultures produced such a meager stock of proverbs surprised him.

VI. What about meaning?

Read the sentences in each list below. In each list there are one or two sentences which have a different meaning from the rest of the sentences. The rest of the sentences on each list all mean the same thing. Draw a line through the sentences which have a different meaning from the rest in their list.

LIST ONE

Look for sentences in this list which do _not_ mean: _Proverbs deal with the fundamental stuff of life. THIS is his idea._ Draw a line through any that you find.

a. That proverbs deal with the fundamental stuff of life is his idea.

b. It is his idea that proverbs deal with the fundamental stuff of life.

c. He has the idea that proverbs deal with the fundamental stuff of life.

d. The idea that he has is that proverbs deal with the fundamental stuff of life.

e. That proverbs deal with the stuff of life is his fundamental idea.

f. He has fundamental proverbs that deal with the stuff of life.

LIST TWO

Look for sentences in this list which do *not* mean: *Wise sayings in different languages sometimes have the same meaning. THIS astonished him.* Draw a line through any that you find.

a. He was astonished by the fact that wise sayings in different languages sometimes have the same meanings.

b. That wise sayings in different languages sometimes have the same meaning astonished him.

c. That wise saying, which sometimes has the same meaning in a different language, is what astonished him.

d. It astonished him that wise sayings in different languages sometimes have the same meaning.

e. For wise sayings in different languages to sometimes have the same idea astonished him.

f. What astonished him was the fact that wise sayings in different languages sometimes have the same meaning.

LIST THREE

Look for sentences in this list which do *not* mean the following: *He recalled SOMETHING. They had a similar proverb.* Draw a line through any that you find.

a. What he recalled was that they had a similar proverb.

b. They recalled his having a similar proverb.

c. He recalled that they had a similar proverb.

d. What he recalled was their having a similar proverb.

e. What they recalled to him was that they had a similar proverb.

f. It was their having a similar proverb that he recalled.

Answers to Sentence Study—Proverbs

NOTE: Whenever *the fact* occurs in parentheses, it is optional.

I. A. 1. (The fact) that wise sayings in different languages sometimes have the same meaning (strikes) (doesn't strike) me as interesting.

2. (The fact) that Milner found proverbs to be a good guide for social life in Samoa (surprised) (didn't surprise) me.

3. (The fact) that different languages have similar sayings (may) (must) indicate that there is a kind of universal wisdom.

4. (The fact) that Milner went to the South Pacific to compile a dictionary indicates his interest in (travel) (language).

5. (The fact) that Milner found a rigidly stratified culture (surprises) (doesn't suprise) me.

6. (The fact) that they had proverbs for every human exchange (intrigues) (doesn't intrigue) me.

7. (The fact) that people share certain feelings about life (implies) (denies) a universal wisdom.

8. (The fact) that proverbs deal in the fundamental stuff of life (should) (should not) surprise us.

NOTE: You might want to compare the words in the parentheses that you underlined with the ones that a classmate underlined and discuss any differences.

B. 1. For Milner to find proverbs to be a good guide for social life in Samoa didn't surprise us.

2. For different languages to have similar sayings may indicate that there is a kind of universal wisdom.

3. Milner's going to the South Pacific to compile a dictionary indicates his interest in language.

4. Milner's finding a rigidly stratified culture surprised some people.

5. (The fact) that they share certain feelings about life implies a universal wisdom.

6. Their having proverbs for every human exchange intrigued him.

7. (The fact) that they deal in the fundamental stuff of life didn't surprise us.

C. Sample answers: (other answers are possible)

1. the fact that he collected so many of them

2. the fact that they had a proverb for every social situation

3. the fact that different languages have similar proverbs

II.   1. It intrigued Milner that they had proverbs for every human exchange.

2. It may be the result of a kind of universal wisdom that proverbs are similar across cultures.

3. It is Milner's idea that proverbs deal with the fundamental stuff of life.

4. It is likely that proverbs in different languages share a common source.

5. It is possible that the universality of human thought is the source of proverbs.

III. A. 1. He mentioned (the fact) that many of the sayings were similar in meaning.

2. He noticed (the fact) that the Samoans used proverbs as a guide for their social life.

3. They forgot (the fact) that the Americans say "Too many cooks spoil the broth."

4. He mentioned (the fact) that some civilizations are rich in proverbs.

B. 1. Did he mention the Samoans having proverbs for every human exchange?

2. Do you recall (the fact) that he compared proverbs from different cultures?

3. Were you aware of his writing that dictionary?

4. He would never deny (the fact) that he was surprised at the similarity of proverbs across cultures.

C. Sample answers:

1. He recalled their having thousands of these pithy sayings.

2. He mentioned (the fact) that the best proverbs have certain characteristics in common.

3. He mentioned (the fact) that every language has its share of proverbs and wise sayings.

4. He recalled (his) having heard a similar proverb in another language.

IV.   1. He supposes that birth and death belong to the fundamental stuff of life.

2. He claims that people share certain feelings about life. (NOTE: *the fact* cannot occur in this sentence.)

3. He recalled (the fact) that the Iranians have a proverb with a meaning like "Too many cooks spoil the broth."

4. He maintained that the best proverbs transcend ethnic and geographic barriers. (NOTE: *the fact* cannot occur in this sentence.)

5. He believes almost every language to have its share of proverbs.

6. One might suppose that all languages have proverbs. But this is not so.

7. He said that no one knows why some people have few proverbs and others have many. (*The fact* cannot occur in this sentence.)

8. He believes proverbs to offer insight into human thought.

9. He supposed the similarity between proverbs to be significant.

10. He mentioned (the fact) that proverbs say a great deal in a very few words.

V. 1. NO He recalled that Milner has collected thousands of proverbs. OR He recalled Milner('s) having collected thousands of proverbs.

   2. OK

   3. NO He believes that people share certain feelings about life.

   4. OK

   5. OK

   6. NO Milner mentioned (the fact) that he was struck by the similarity of proverbs across cultures. OR Milner mentioned (the fact of) his being struck by the similarity of proverbs across cultures.

   7. OK

   8. OK

   9. OK

  10. NO That proverbs provide a clue to the common denominator of all human thought is unlikely.

  11. OK

  12. NO He said that the Arabs minted many proverbs.

  13. OK

  14. NO (The fact) that some cultures produced such a meager stock of proverbs surprised him.

VI. *List One*—Draw lines through e and f

    List Two—Draw a line through c

    List Three—Draw lines through b and e

Folk Medicine

Turning Sentences into Complements:
To, Passives, and Split Sentences

OVERVIEW

I. Turning sentences into complements by using *to* [*urge him to go, etc.*] and the passive paraphrase. Verbs: *urge, ask, order, advise, permit, encourage, persuade, allow, compel, force, help.*

II. Turning sentences into complements by using *to* [*want (him) to go, etc.*] and the split sentence paraphrase. Verbs: *want, prefer, like, wish.*

III. *From + ing* after *prevent, stop, keep* [*prevent him from _____ing, etc.*].

IV. Summary exercise.

V. What about meaning?

I. Turning sentences into complements by using *to* [*urge him to go, etc.*] and the passive paraphrase. Verbs: *urge, ask, order, advise, permit, encourage, persuade, allow, compel, force, help.*

A. Combine each pair of sentences below as in the example. Also underline one of the expressions in parentheses (according to the sense of the reading and listening texts.)

Example: His grandmother advised him ~~TO DO SOMETHING.~~

~~He should~~ *to* wear a sack of (asafoetida) (rose petals).

Do not copy the sentence. Just delete and add, as illustrated in the example.

1. Circumstances compelled primitive man TO DO SOMETHING.

   He should find his remedies in (nature) (drugstores).

2. A string of Job's Tears (can) (cannot) help a child TO DO

  SOMETHING. He should cut his teeth.

3. (Rheumatism) (Fever) forced the animal TO DO SOMETHING.

  He must seek a spot of hot sunlight.

4. Practitioners of folk medicine (urge) (do not urge) people TO

  DO SOMETHING. They should condition the body in its

  entirety.

5. You (can) (can't) force a person TO DO SOMETHING. He

  should take medicine.

6. Fern roots can help (a wild turkey) (a bear) DO SOMETHING.

  He can overcome sickness.

7. Chewing (fern roots) (snakeroot) permits an animal TO DO

  SOMETHING. He can avoid death from snakebite.

AFTER HELP, as in sentences 2 and 6 above, the *to* can be omitted: *They help a child (to) cut his teeth.*

B. Write a passive paraphrase for 7 of the 8 sentences below. One of the sentences cannot be changed into a meaningful passive paraphrase. Which one is it? Write its number here: _____

  Example: His grandmother advised him to wear a sack of asafoetida.

  He was advised (by his grandmother) to wear a sack of asafoetida.

Place the by-phrase in parentheses to show that it can be omitted, as it commonly is.

1. Circumstances compelled primitive man to find his remedies in nature.

   _____

2. A string of Job's Tears cannot help a child (to) cut his teeth.

   _____

3. Rheumatism forced the animal to seek a spot of sunlight.

   _____

4. Practitioners of folk medicine urge people to condition the body in its entirety.

   _____

5. You can't force a person to take medicine.
                              (by anyone)

   _____

6. Fern roots can help (a wild turkey) (a bear) (to) overcome sickness.

   _____

7. Chewing snakeroot permits an animal to avoid death from snakebite.

   _____

   _____

AFTER HELP, as in sentences 2 and 6 above, the *to* can be omitted in the active sentence, but not in the passive sentence.

C. Rewrite each of the following sentences, saying the same thing in a different way. The first one is done as an example.

   1. You can be helped (by nature) to cure your sickness.

      Nature can help you cure your sickness.

   2. The boy was asked (by his grandmother) to collect some Job's Tears.

      _____

   3. Primitive man was forced (by circumstances) to depend on nature for medicines.

      _____

II. Turning sentences into complements by using *to* [*want (him) to go,* etc.*]* and the split sentence paraphrase. Verbs: *want, prefer, like, wish*.

   A. Combine each pair of sentences below as in the examples. Also underline one of the expressions in parentheses (according to the sense of the reading and listening texts).

   Example: She prefers ~~SOMETHING.~~ *(for)* ʌHer child ~~should~~ *to*ʌ (wear) (make) a string of Job's Tears. (NOTE: *for* is optional.)

   Do not copy the sentence. Just delete and add, as illustrated in the examples.

   1. His grandmother would like SOMETHING. He should (carry) (wear) a sack of asafoetida to school.   (*for* is optional)

   2. An animal wants SOMETHING. His rheumatism should (go away) (come back).   (do not use *for* after want)

   3. (All) (Some) people would like SOMETHING. Nature should provide their only medicine.   (*for* is optional)

   4. They (want) (do not want) SOMETHING. People should condition the body in its entirety.   (do not use *for* after *want*)

   5. A wild turkey wants SOMETHING. Her babies should eat leaves of the spice bush during (a rainy spell) (warm weather). (do not use *for* after *want*)

   Example: The animal wants ~~SOMETHING. It should~~ *to*ʌ (seek) (avoid) a spot of sunlight.

   6. (Practitioners of) (People who object to) folk medicine prefer SOMETHING. They should find their remedies in nature.

7. A child (likes) (doesn't like) SOMETHING. He should wear a sack of asafoetida.

8. A mother (wishes) (doesn't wish) SOMETHING. She should help her child cut his teeth.

B. Turn each of the following sentences into a split sentence by placing *What* in front of the sentence and *is for* after the first verb, as in the example.

Example: *What is for* She prefers ∧ (for) her child to wear a string of Job's Tears.

1. His grandmother would like (for) him to wear a sack of asafoetida to school.

2. An animal wants his rheumatism to go away.

3. Some people would like (for) Nature to provide their only medicine.

4. They want people to condition the body in its entirety.

5. A wild turkey wants her babies to eat leaves of the spice bush during a rainy spell.

6. Practitioners of folk medicine prefer to find their remedies in nature.   (do not use *for*—use only *is*)

7. A child doesn't like to wear a sack of asafoetida.   (do not use *for*—use only *is*)

8. A mother wishes to help her child cut his teeth.   (do not use *for*—use only *is*)

NOTICE THAT in sentences 6, 7, and 8 the verb is followed directly by a *to*-expression. There is no noun or pronoun between the verb and the *to*. In such a case *for* does not occur.

C. Rewrite each of the following sentences, saying the same thing in a different way. The first is done as an example.

1. What the animal wanted was to find a spot of sunlight.

   The animal wanted to find a spot of sunlight.

2. What practitioners of folk medicine prefer is for people to condition the body in its entirety.

   _____

   _____

3. What they prefer is to depend on nature for medicines.

   _____

   _____

4. What he didn't want was for his mother to make him wear a sack of asafoetida.

   _____

   _____

III. *From + ing* after *prevent, stop, keep* (*prevent him from* ———*ing,* etc.)

   To prevent someone from SOMETHING, to stop one from SOME-THING, and *to keep one from SOMETHING* have a negative meaning. They mean that something is NOT done.

   A. Combine each pair of sentences below as in the example. Also underline one of the expressions in parentheses (according to the sense of the reading and listening texts).

   Example: They thought that asafoetida kept one from ~~SOME-~~

   ~~THING. One would~~ get *ting* (sick) (well).

   Do not copy the sentence. Just delete and add, as in the example.

   1. They tried to prevent the children from SOMETHING. They

      would (remove) (eat) the Job's Tears that they were wearing.

   2. Rheumatism prevented the animal from SOMETHING. It would

      (hide) (hunt) food.

   3. Some folk remedies may keep you from SOMETHING. You

      would get (sick) (well).

4. There (may be) (should be) no way to prevent a poisonous snake from SOMETHING. He would bite an animal.

5. Chewing snakeroot keeps an animal from SOMETHING. It would die of (snakebite) (hunger).

6. (Eating) (Wearing) leaves from the spice bush keeps baby wild turkeys from SOMETHING. They would get sick in rainy weather.

7. There are healing plants which can keep animals from SOME-THING. They would (get well) (suffer).

8. You (must) (cannot) stop people from SOMETHING. They would look for cures.

COMPARE THESE two sentences: *This medicine will keep you from getting sick. This medicine will keep you well. Keep* can be used to express the maintaining of a state, as in the second sentence. Other examples: *This blanket will keep you warm. The toy will keep the child happy. The problem has kept her upset for several days.*

B. Rewrite each of the following sentences, saying the same thing in a different way. The first one is done for you as an example. (NOTE: What you will be doing is changing passive voice to active voice.)

1. He was stopped from picking Job's Tears by the old man.

   The old man stopped him from picking Job's Tears.

2. They were kept from getting well by the lack of medicine.

   _____

3. She was prevented from taking off the sack of asafoetida by her teacher.

   _____

   _____

4. The fever was kept from rising by the application of ice packs.

_____

_____

5. Were you ever prevented from taking folk medicine (by any-one)?

_____

_____

C. Put together five sentences, using the following parts. For each sentence that you put together, take the first part from X, the second part from Y, and the third part from Z. Notice that you must turn the phrases from Z into *ing*-expressions.

X: the doctor   Y: prevented him from
     bad weather   kept him from
     now nothing   could stop him from
     you   can't stop people from
     the herb medicine

     Z: he would find the herbs
          he would take the medicine
          they would believe myths about folk medicine
          he would get sick
          he would get well

Example: Bad weather   kept him from   getting well.
               (X)   (Y)   (Z)

1. _____

_____

2. _____

_____

3. _____

_____

4. _____

_____

5. _____

_____

IV. Summary Exercise. Put OK in front of each sentence that you con-sider correct. Put NO in front of each sentence that you consider incorrect and then correct it. The first one is done as an example.

_No_   1. His grandmother asked him ^to^ wear a string of Job's Tears.

_____ 2. What they would prefer is for nature to cure them.

_____ 3. They prevented the snake to bite the child.

——————— 4. People can be helped get well.

——————— 5. The father advised to pick some herbs.

——————— 6. They urged the people to maintain health and vigor.

——————— 7. He was wanted by the doctor to take some medicine.

——————— 8. Herbs can help people get well.

——————— 9. What they wanted was for the bear to find fern roots.

——————— 10. This medicine will keep you from sick.

V. What about meaning?

In each sentence below, underline the word that refers to the person who would go. The first one is done as an example.

1. He urged me to go. (I would go.)
2. They wanted to go.
3. He was forced by them to go.
4. Was she asked to go?
5. What they would like is for him to go.
6. Was he compelled by them to go?
7. Did they permit her to go?
8. Was he persuaded by his friends to go?
9. What he wanted was to go with her.
10. They were ordered to go by their supervisor.

Answers to Sentence Study—Folk Medicine

I. A.   Look at the sentences in B (p. 96). They are the same as the sentences that you should write for A.

B. 1. Primitive man was compelled (by circumstances) to find his remedies in nature.

2. A child cannot be helped (by a string of Job's Tears) to cut his teeth.

3. The animal was forced (by rheumatism) to seek a spot of hot sunlight.

4. People are urged (by practitioners of folk medicine) to condition the body in its entirety.

5. A person can't be forced (by anyone) to take medicine.

6. A bear can be helped (by fern roots) to overcome illness.

7. The passive is not a meaningful paraphrase for this sentence. The reason is that *chewing snakeroot*, which is the subject of *permits*, cannot give permission. That is, an animal cannot be permitted by *chewing snakeroot* to avoid death from snakebite.

C. 1. Nature can help you (to) cure your sicknesses.

   2. The boy's grandmother asked him to collect some Job's Tears.

   3. Circumstances forced primitive man to depend on nature for medicines.

II. A. Look at the sentences in B (p. 99). They are the same as the sentences that you should write for A.

   B. 1. What his grandmother would like is for him to wear a sack of asafoetida to school.

   2. What an animal wants is for his rheumatism to go away.

   3. What some people would like is for Nature to provide their only medicine.

   4. What they want is for people to condition the body in its entirety.

   5. What a wild turkey wants is for her babies to eat leaves of the spice bush during a rainy spell.

   6. What practitioners of folk medicine prefer is to find their remedies in nature.

   7. What a child doesn't like is to wear a sack of asafoetida.

   8. What a mother wishes is to help her child cut his teeth.

   C. 1. The animal wanted to find a spot of hot sunlight.

   2. Practitioners of folk medicine prefer (for) people to condition the body in its entirety.

   3. They prefer to depend on nature for medicines.

   4. He didn't want his mother to make him wear a sack of asafoetida.

III. A. 1. They tried to prevent the children from removing the Job's Tears that they were wearing.

   2. Rheumatism prevented the animal from hunting food.

   3. Some folk remedies may keep you from getting sick.

   4. There may be no way to prevent a poisonous snake from biting an animal.

   5. Chewing snakeroot keeps an animal from dying of snakebite.

   6. Eating leaves from the spice bush keeps baby wild turkeys from getting sick in rainy weather.

7. There are healing plants which can keep animals from suffering.

8. You can't stop people from looking for cures.

B. 1. The old man stopped him from picking Job's Tears.

2. The lack of medicine kept them from getting well.

3. Her teacher prevented her from taking off the sack of asafoetida.

4. The application of ice packs kept the fever from rising.

5. Did anyone ever prevent you from taking folk medicine?

C. Sample answers (other answers are possible):
The herb medicine kept him from getting sick.
You can't stop people from believing myths about folk medicine.
Now nothing could stop him from taking the medicine.
You could stop him from getting sick.

IV. 1. NO His grandmother asked him *to* wear a string of Job's Tears.

2. OK

3. NO They prevented the snake *from biting* the child.

4. NO People can be helped *to* get well.

5. NO The father advised someone (him, her, them, etc.) to pick some herbs.

6. OK

7. NO The doctor wanted him to take some medicine. (The passive is not possible.)

8. OK

9. OK

10. NO This medicine will keep you from *getting* (OR *becoming*) sick.

V. 1. me

2. they

3. he

4. she

5. him

6. he

7. her

8. he

9. he

10. they

Nonverbal Communication

Turning Sentences into Complements:
(For) To and That

OVERVIEW

I. Turning sentences into complements by using *(for) to—prefer to do, prefer (for) him to do*, etc. Verbs: *prefer, like, want, wish, plan, hope, expect.*

II. Turning sentences into complements by using *to* and sometimes *that—He expected to go; He expected that he would go*, etc. Verbs: *prefer, like, want, wish, plan, hope, expect, promise, decide, resolve, remember, forget.*

III. Summary exercise.

IV. What about meaning?

I. Turning sentences into complements by using *(for) to* (with and without a noun/pronoun in front of *to*)—*prefer to do, prefer (for) him to do*, etc. Verbs: *prefer, like, want, wish, plan, hope, expect.* Combine each pair of sentences below, as in the examples.

Examples: He prefers ~~SOMETHING. He~~ stand*s̸* ^*to*^ close to the person

he is speaking to. (Notice that the subjects of the two sentences are the same.)

optional → (for)
Some cultures prefer ~~SOMETHING.~~ ^ Their members

^*to*^ stand close to each other when speaking. (Notice that the subjects of the sentences are different.)

Do not copy the sentences. Just delete and add, as in the examples.

1. The speaker wishes SOMETHING. The audience would move further front.

2. They want SOMETHING. The man who went to the party would report his observations. (Do not use *for*)

3. They were hoping for SOMETHING. The crowd would cheer.

4. He expects SOMETHING. The speaker will explain cultural variations in eye contact.

5. He hopes SOMETHING. He will observe the speaker's gestures.

6. He wants SOMETHING. He would signal her across the crowded room.

7. He expects SOMETHING. He will go to the party.

8. He likes SOMETHING. He observes her gestures.

9. He wishes SOMETHING. He would explain why North Americans are often considered ''cold.''

10. He prefers SOMETHING. People would look at him when they talk to him.

II. Turning sentences into complements by using *to* and sometimes *that* (except after *prefer, like,* and *want*)—*He expected to go; He expected that he would go,* etc. Verbs: *prefer, like, want, wish, plan, hope, expect, promise, decide, resolve, remember, forget.*

   A. Verbs like the ones just listed describe a mental state which comes before an action. The meaning of such a verb is that the action named by the *to*-expression (which comes after the verb) *may* perhaps happen, but there is no certainty that it actually will happen.

   Combine each pair of sentences below, as in the example. In each sentence which has a pair of expressions in parentheses, you are to underline the one which fits the sense of the reading and listening texts OR the one which is your own choice. Not all the sentences have such pairs of expressions.

Example: The (North) (South) American prefers ~~SOMETHING.~~

~~He would~~ _^*to* keep distance between himself and the

person he is talking to.

Do not copy the sentences. Just delete and add, as in the example.

1. I (like) (don't like) SOMETHING. I would observe nonverbal

    communication.

2. In (North) (South) America people expect SOMETHING.

    They will stand close to each other when speaking.

3. He promised SOMETHING. He would explain cultural vari-

    ations in eye contact.

4. He resolved SOMETHING. He would see if he could get her

    to look him in the eye.

5. She planned SOMETHING. She would flirt with him by looking

    him in the eye.

6. He doesn't wish SOMETHING. He would discomfit his friends

    with too much smiling.

7. I (hope) (don't want) SOMETHING. I will learn more about

    nonverbal communication.

8. Remember SOMETHING. Think of the significance of physical

    distance when speaking to someone.

9. You shouldn't forget SOMETHING. You should notice people's

    silent language.

10. In the Middle East, a girl does not want SOMETHING. She
will not let a young man catch her eye, unless she is being
extremely (shy) (flirtatious).

NOTE: Both *prefer* and *like* can be followed by *ing*-expressions as well as
by *to*-expressions. For example: *He prefers to observe nonverbal communication. He prefers observing nonverbal communication.* When the *ing*-
expression is used the meaning is that he does in fact observe nonverbal
communication. When the *to*-expression is used the meaning is that maybe
he did observe and maybe he didn't.

Forget and *decide* may be followed either by a *to*-expression or by a preposition plus an *ing*-expression: *forget to go/forget about going; decide to
go/decide on going.*

Remember and *forget* can also be followed by *ing*-expressions: *He remembered to go.* (The going comes after the remembering.) *He remembered
going.* (The remembering comes after the going.) *He forgot to mail the
letter.* (He didn't mail the letter.) *He forgot mailing the letter.* (He mailed
the letter.)

B. Rewrite the complements in the sentences below by changing
the *to*-expression into a *that*-expression, as in the example.

Example:
He didn't expect *to discomfit the other people with his smiling.*

  *that he would discomfit the
  other people with his smiling.*

1. The scientists decided *to observe nonverbal communication
at parties.*

   _____

2. They hoped *to find the part that eyes play in nonverbal communication.*

   _____

3. He resolved *to study eye contact in different cultures.*

   _____

4. He decided *to stand closer to her.*

   _____

5. He doesn't expect *to understand all the gestures.*

_____

_____

6. She planned *not to look him in the eye.*

_____

_____

7. She promised *not to smile too much.*

_____

_____

8. Scientists hope *to help cultures understand each other better.*

_____

_____

NOTICE THAT after *plan, hope, expect, promise, decide,* and *resolve,* a *to*-expression can sometimes be paraphrased by a *that*-expression as in the sentences above.

C. A *that*-expression can occur after *wish, plan, hope, expect, promise, decide, resolve, remember,* and *forget.* Sometimes it is a paraphrase of the *to*-expression and sometimes it isn't.

In the sentences below, change the *that*-expression into a *to*-expression wherever it is possible to do so without changing the meaning. Where it is not possible to do so without changing the meaning, write *not possible* in the blank.

Examples:
I expect *that I will be there.*
    to be there
I expect *that I should have gone.*
    not possible

1. In South America people expect *that they will stand close to each other when speaking.*

_____

2. Don't forget *that you should notice people's silent language.*

_____

3. She hopes *that she will learn more about nonverbal communication.*

_____

4. She decided *that she would flirt with him by looking him in the eye.*

_____

5. Remember *that you might misinterpret eye movements.*

_____

6. He promised *that he would explain cultural variations in eye contact.*

   _____

7. He resolved *that he would see if he could get her to look him in the eye.*

   _____

8. He forgot *that he would offend people by standing too close to them.*

   _____

9. Remember *that you should pay attention to physical distance when speaking to people.*

   _____

10. He wished *that he could explain why South Americans seem "pushy."*

    _____

11. He had planned *that he would go to the party.*

    _____

12. She decided *that she had flirted with him unintentionally.*

    _____

III. Summary exercise. Put OK in front of each sentence that you consider correct. Put NO in front of each sentence that you consider incorrect and then correct it. The first one is done as an example.

   No   1. He wanted ~~for~~ to catch her eye.

   _____ 2. Susan decided looking him in the eye.

   _____ 3. He remembered that she looked down frequently.

   _____ 4. The teacher resolved to study the silent language of his students.

   _____ 5. She hopes them to continue their study of nonverbal communication.

   _____ 6. He wanted to catch her eye.

   _____ 7. James decided her to go with him.

   _____ 8. She hopes for them to continue their study of nonverbal communication.

   _____ 9. He remembered her to look down frequently.

   _____ 10. James decided that she should go with him.

   _____ 11. The lecturer forgot to mention the differences in physical distance in different cultures.

   _____ 12. The teacher resolved studying the silent language of his students.

   _____ 13. Susan decided to look him in the eye.

   _____ 14. She prefers talking with a person who will look her in the eye.

_____ 15. The lecturer forgot mentioning the differences in physical distance between cultures.

IV. What about meaning?

In each item below, put an X in front of the sentence on the right which you think is the closest in meaning to the sentence on the left. In one item, both of the sentences on the right are equally close to the meaning of the sentence on the left, and so both should be marked X.

1. He doesn't wish her to be considered flirtatious.

_____ a. He doesn't wish that she be considered flirtatious.

_____ b. He doesn't wish her to consider him flirtatious.

2. They decided to observe gestures as their project.

_____ a. They decided on observing gestures as their project.

_____ b. They decided that they would observe gestures as their project.

3. She promised to observe his gestures.

_____ a. She promised him to observe his gestures.

_____ b. She promised that she would observe his gestures.

4. They prefer to stand close when they talk.

_____ a. They prefer them to stand close when they talk.

_____ b. They prefer standing close when they talk.

5. He hadn't expected to look her in the eye.

_____ a. He hadn't expected that he would look her in the eye.

_____ b. He hadn't expected her to look him in the eye.

6. He forgot to shake hands with her.

_____ a. He forgot shaking hands with her.

_____ b. He didn't shake hands with her because he forgot to.

7. They decided on going.

_____ a. They decided that they would go.

——— b. They decided that they
could go.

8. She remembered having   ——— a. She remembered that
flirted with him.   she had flirted with him.
——— b. She remembered to
flirt with him.

Answers to Sentence Study—Nonverbal Communication

I.   1. The speaker wishes the audience to move further front.
2. They want the man who went to the party to report his observations.
3. They were hoping for the crowd to cheer.
4. He expects (for) the speaker to explain cultural variations in eye contact. (In some dialects the *for* may be unacceptable.)
5. He hopes to observe the speaker's gestures.
6. He wants to signal her across the crowded room.
7. He expects to go to the party.
8. He likes to observe her gestures.
9. He wishes to explain why North Americans are often considered "cold."
10. He prefers (for) people to look at him when they talk to him.

II. A. 1. I (like) (don't like) to observe nonverbal communication. Underline your choice
2. In South America people expect to stand close to each other when speaking.
3. He promised to explain cultural variations in eye contact.
4. He resolved to see if he could get her to look him in the eye.
5. She planned to flirt with him by looking him in the eye.
6. He doesn't wish to discomfit his friends with too much smiling.
7. I (hope) (don't want) to learn more about nonverbal communication. Underline your choice
8. Remember to think of the significance of physical distance when speaking to someone.
9. You shouldn't forget to notice people's silent language.
10. In the Middle East, a girl does not want to let a young man catch her eye, unless she is being extremely flirtatious.

B. 1. The scientists decided that they would observe nonverbal communication at parties.

2. They hoped that they would find the part that eyes play in nonverbal communication.

3. He resolved that he would study eye contact in different cultures.

4. He decided that he would stand closer to her.

5. He doesn't expect that he will understand all the gestures.

6. She planned that she would not look him in the eye.

7. She promised that she would not smile too much.

8. Scientists hope that they will help cultures understand each other better.

C. 1. In South America people expect to stand close to each other when speaking.

2. Don't forget to notice people's silent language.

3. She hopes to learn more about nonverbal communication.

4. She decided to flirt with him by looking him in the eye.

5. Not possible (without a change in meaning)

6. He promised to explain cultural variations in eye contact.

7. He resolved to see if he could get her to look him in the eye.

8. Not possible (without a change in meaning)

9. Remember to pay attention to physical distance when speaking to people.

10. Not possible (without a change in meaning)

11. He had planned to go to the party.

12. Not possible (without a change in meaning)

III.   1. NO He wanted to catch her eye.

2. NO Susan decided to look him in the eye. (OR Susan decided on looking him in the eye. This suggests that she made a decision between looking him in the eye and something else.)

3. OK

4. OK

5. NO She hopes for them to continue their study of nonverbal communication. (OR She hopes that they will continue their study of nonverbal communication.)

6. OK

7. NO James decided that she should go with him.

8. OK

9. NO He remembered that she looked down frequently.

10. OK

11. OK

12. NO The teacher resolved to study the silent language of his students.

13. OK

14. OK

15. OK (The meaning is that the lecturer mentioned the differences and then forgot the fact that he had mentioned them.)

IV.   1. a

2. a, b

3. b

4. b

5. a

6. b

7. a

8. a

Intelligence

Turning Sentences into Subjects and Objects:
That and Whether or Not

OVERVIEW

I. Turning sentences into objects by using *that* and *whether or not.*

II. Saying the same thing with a *that*-expression and an *ing*-expression.

III. Changing sentences with *that*-expression objects into passive. Changing passives into sentences beginning with *it.*

IV. Changing sentences with *that*-expression subjects into sentences beginning with *it.*

V. Summary exercise.

IV. What about meanings?

I. Turning sentences into objects by using *that* and *whether or not.*

A. Fill in the blank in each sentence with *whether or not* or *that*, or, if both are possible, write in both. (There are three sentences, including the first one, which can take both.) The first two sentences are done as examples.

1. Holt doesn't mention *whether or not* it is possible to teach dull children to experiment.

2. Holt mentions (the fact) ___*that*___ the intelligent person opens himself up to a new situation.

3. Did you notice _____ Holt mentioned that a few children are born with problems?

4. Holt has noticed (the fact) _____ the dull child sticks more to himself and his own dream world.

5. A bright child often wonders _____ there is another way that might work.

6. A bright child keeps on trying even though he doesn't always know _____ he can find a solution.

7. He says _____ a bright child can learn from his mistakes.

8. He maintains _____ the dull child is usually afraid to try at all.

9. Some people think _____ scores on IQ tests indicate intelligence.

10. Holt doesn't think _____ the schools are doing a good job of educating children.

11. A bright child feels _____ there's more than one way to skin a cat.

12. He concludes _____ the child is not at fault.

IN THE SENTENCES where both *that* and *whether or not* can occur, the use of the *that*-expression means that the idea conveyed by the *that*-expression is true, and the use of the *whether or not* expression means that the idea conveyed by the *whether or not* expression is open to question. For example:

> Holt doesn't mention that it is possible to teach dull children to experiment. (Meaning: It is possible to teach dull children to experiment but Holt doesn't mention that fact.)

> Holt doesn't mention whether or not it is possible to teach dull children to experiment. (Meaning: Is it possible to teach dull children to experiment? Holt doesn't answer this question.)

AS A GENERAL RULE, *that* can be deleted when the *that*-expression follows the verb, as it does in the above sentences. Deletion of *that* makes the sentence more informal. Example: *Holt probably hopes the schools will improve.*

AFTER THE VERBS *mention* and *notice*, the *that*-expression can optionally be preceded by *the fact*. Example: *Holt mentions the fact that the intelligent person opens himself up to a new situation.*

NOTICE THE FOLLOWING VARIATIONS of the *whether or not* expression. The sentences below all mean the same thing.

I wonder *whether or not* he knows the answer.

I wonder *whether* he knows the answer *or not*.

I wonder *whether* he knows the answer.

I wonder *if* he knows the answer.

B. Using the following subjects, verbs, and sentences, put together three sentences of your own. You must turn each sentence that you choose from the list of sentences into a *that*-expression or a *whether or not* expression. Make your sentences true according to the listening text.

Subjects: Holt, a bright child

Verbs: think, mention, believe, feel, wonder

Sentences: A child learns a lot in the first three years of his life.
There is more than one way of doing things.
Scores on IQ tests don't show intelligence.
There isn't just one way to skin a cat.
The schools do not help children grow intellectually.

Example: *Holt feels that scores on IQ Tests don't show intelligence.*

1. _____

2. _____

3. _____

Using the following subjects, verbs and sentences, put together more sentences of your own in the same way that you did above. Make your sentences true according to the listening text.

Subjects: Holt, a bright child

Verbs: do not think, do not mention, do not believe, do not feel

Sentences: Things will work out.
The schools will change.
Scores on IQ tests show intelligence.
There's only one way to skin a cat.
The schools help children grow intellectually.

Example: *Holt does not mention whether or not the schools will change.*

4. _____

5. _____

6. _____

C. Put together three more sentences in the same way as you did above, using any of the subjects, verbs, and sentences listed in B. This time, make up sentences that are *not* true, according to the listening text.

1. _____

2. _____
_____
3. _____
_____

II. Saying the same thing with a *that*-expression and an *ing*-expression.

A. In each of the sentence sequences below, turn the second sentence into (a) a *that*-expression and (b) an *ing*-expression, as in the example.

Example:

(a) Holt mentions ~~SOMETHING.~~ *(the fact) that* ~~T~~hey don't experiment.

(b) Holt mentions ~~SOMETHING. They don't~~ experiment. *their not* *ing.*

Do not copy the sentences. Just add and delete, as in the example.

In all the sentences below which contain *that*-expressions, *the fact* is optional.

1. (a) Holt notices SOMETHING. He tries to get in touch with

   everything around him.

   (b) Holt notices SOMETHING. He tries to get in touch with

   everything around him.

2. (a) Holt deplores SOMETHING. They turn out dull.

   (b) Holt deplores SOMETHING. They turn out dull.

3. (a) Holt mentions SOMETHING. We don't start out dull.

   (b) Holt mentions SOMETHING. We don't start out dull.

4. (a) Holt regrets SOMETHING. We lose our ability to learn.

   (b) Holt regrets SOMETHING. We lose our ability to learn.

5. (a) Holt notices SOMETHING. There are actually two different

   kinds of people.

(b) Holt notices SOMETHING. There are actually two different

kinds of people.

B. In each item below, a meaning is expressed in one way (using either a *that*-expression or an *ing*-expression). On the blank line, write the other way of expressing the meaning. Also, indicate who or what the pronoun refers to. (You can find out by looking in the reading or listening texts: L-2 = Listening Text, paragraph 2, etc.; R-2 = Reading Text, paragraph 2, and so forth). The first one is done as an example.

1. Holt mentions (the fact) that they aren't sure how it will all work out.

   Holt mentions their not being sure how it will all work out.

   (L-2) they = *intelligent persons (or people)*

2. Holt notices his looking without shame or fear at his mistakes.

   _____

   _____

   (R-2) he = _____

3. Holt regrets (the fact) that he does not try to find a way that works.

   _____

   _____

   (L-5) he = _____

4. Holt is aware of their having a special outlook on life.
   (delete *of*) _____

   _____

   (L-2) they = _____

5. Holt deplores its destroying the ability to learn.
   (add *the fact*) _____

   _____

   (L-7) its = _____

6. Holt mentions (the fact) that he experiments.

   _____

   _____

   (L-5) he = _____

C. Make up four sentences of your own like those in A and B above. In your sentences use only the verbs that are used in the sentences in A and B. In two of your sentences use a *that*-expression. In the other two use an *ing*-expression. Ask a classmate or your teacher to check your sentences for you.

1. _____
   _____
2. _____
   _____
3. _____
   _____
4. _____
   _____

III. Changing sentences with *that*-expression objects into the passive. Changing the passives into sentences beginning with *it*.

  A. The first five sentences below can be changed into the passive by reversing the subject and object and making appropriate changes in the verb. Then, as a second step, the *that*-expression can be moved to the end of the sentence and an *it* can take its place as subject. Your task is to do the second step in each item below. The first one is done as an example.

  1. He mentions (the fact) that IQ tests are only indicators of intelligence.
     Step 1: (The fact) that IQ Tests are only indicators of intelligence is mentioned.
     Step 2: *It is mentioned that IO tests are only indicators of intelligence.*

  2. He noted (the fact) that the bright child tries to get in touch with everything.
     Step 1: (The fact) that the bright child tries to get in touch with everything was noted.
     Step 2: _____

  3. He takes into account (the fact) that we don't start out dull.
     Step 1: (The fact) that we don't start out dull is taken into account.
     Step 2: _____

  4. He deplores (the fact) that we lose our ability to learn.
     Step 1: (The fact) that we lose our ability to learn is to be deplored.
     Step 2: _____

  5. He regrets (the fact) that the dull child doesn't experiment.
     Step 1: That the dull child doesn't experiment is to be regretted.
     Step 2: _____

  In the sentences that you have just completed Step 2 is optional. In the five sentences below, however, Step 2 is necessary. If you stop at Step 1, the sentence that you have is un-grammatical. The Step 1 sentences below are marked with an asterisk (*), which means that they are ungrammatical.

Your task is to write out Step 2 for each sentence. Sentence 6 is done as an example. Notice that in these sentences it is not possible to insert *the fact* in front of the *that*-expression. If you put it in you will end up with an ungrammatical sentence.

6. He hopes that the schools will change.
   Step 1: *That the schools will change is hoped.
   Step 2: *It is hoped that the schools will change.*

7. He believes that there are actually two different kinds of people.
   Step 1: *That there are actually two different kinds of people is believed.
   Step 2: _____

8. He says that we lose our ability to learn.
   Step 1: *That we lose our ability to learn is said.
   Step 2: _____

9. He claims that the bright child wants to find out about life.
   Step 1: *That the bright child wants to find out about life is claimed.
   Step 2: _____

10. He supposes that "unintelligence" is not just a smaller amount of intelligence.
    Step 1: *That "unintelligence" is not just a smaller amount of intelligence is supposed.
    Step 2: _____

B. Fill in the blank in each of the sentences below with one of these items: *made clear, supposed, claimed, deplored, required.* Although some of the blanks can be filled with more than one of the choices, you are asked to choose one item for each blank and use each item only once. Choose items according to the sense of the reading and listening texts. The first sentence is done as an example.

   1. That a bright child will experiment when he gets into trouble was *made clear*.

   2. That schools destroy the ability to learn is to be
      _____ .

   3. It is _____ that bright children have a special outlook on life.

4. It is to be _____ that the dull child doesn't try to find a way that works.

5. It is commonly _____ that schools help children grow intellectually.

C. All the sentences in B above are passive. Rewrite each of them as active sentences. The first one is done as an example.

1. *He makes it clear that a bright child will experiment when he gets into trouble.*

   (NOTE: When the *that*-expression comes after *make clear, it* must occur between *make* and *clear*.)

2. _____

3. _____

4. _____

5. _____

IV. Changing sentences with *that*-expressions as subjects into sentences beginning with *it*.

A. Notice these two ways of saying the same thing:

   (1) That a person starts off stupid is unlikely.

   (2) It is unlikely that a person starts off stupid.

   In each item below, something is said in one way. On the blank line, write in the other way of saying the same thing. The first one is done as an example.

   1. It is probable that education destroys our ability to learn.

   That education destroys our ability to learn is probable.

   2. That an intelligent person tries to find out all he can about a new situation is likely.

   _____

   _____

   3. That there is more than one way to skin a cat is certain.

   _____

   _____

   4. It is uncertain whether the schools will change or not.

   _____

   _____

   5. That adults will ever learn as much in three years as a child is improbable.

   _____

   _____

6. It is likely that an intelligent person has a special outlook on life.

_____

_____

7. That a bright child will try to solve a difficult problem in only one way is unlikely.

_____

_____

8. It is certain that education is supposed to take place in school.

_____

_____

B. Using the following adjectives and sentences, put together three statements beginning with _it_. You will need to turn the sentences into _that_-expressions.

Adjectives: likely, probable, certain

Sentences: When a bright child gets into trouble he will experiment.

There is a difference between "bright" and "not bright" children.

Most dull children are not born dull.

"Unintelligence" is not just a smaller amount of intelligence.

Example: _It is probable that, when a bright child gets into trouble, he will experiment._

1. _____

_____

2. _____

_____

3. _____

_____

Using the following adjectives and sentences, put together three more statements beginning with _it_. You will need to turn the sentences into either _that_-expressions or _whether or not_ expressions.

Adjectives: unlikely (use _that_)

improbable (use _that_)

uncertain (use _whether or not_)

Sentences: Most children are born dull.

He doesn't think that the schools are doing
a good job.   YES   NO

9. He noticed the fact that dull children don't
experiment.
He didn't notice the fact that dull children
experiment.   YES   NO

10. He mentioned the fact that the dull child
doesn't want to find out about life.
He didn't mention the fact that the dull child
wants to find out about life.   YES   NO

Answers to Sentence Study—Intelligence

I. A. 1. that, whether or not
2. that
3. that, whether or not
4. that
5. whether or not
6. that, whether or not
7. that
8. that
9. that
10. that
11. that
12. that

B. Examples: (other sentences are possible)

Holt feels that the schools do not help children grow intellectually.

A bright child thinks that there is more than one way of doing things.

A bright child wonders whether or not there is more than one way of doing things.

Holt does not believe that scores on IQ tests show intelligence.

A bright child does not feel that there's only one way to skin a cat.

Holt does not mention whether or not things will work out.

C. Examples: (other sentences are possible)

Holt believes that the schools help children grow intellectually.

A bright child thinks there's only one way to skin a cat.

Holt does not believe that a child learns a lot in the first three years of his life.

II. A. 1(a) Holt notices that he tries to get in touch with everything around him.

    (b) Holt notices his trying to get in touch with everything around him.

    2(a) Holt deplores the fact that they turn out dull.

    (b) Holt deplores their turning out dull.

    3(a) Holt mentions that we don't start out dull.

    (b) Holt mentions our not starting out dull.

    4(a) Holt regrets that we lose our ability to learn.

    (b) Holt regrets our losing our ability to learn.

    5(a) Holt notices that there are actually two different kinds of people.

    (b) Holt notices there being actually two different kinds of people.

  B. 1. Holt mentions their not being sure how it will all work out.
they = intelligent persons (or people)

    2. Holt notices (the fact) that he looks without shame or fear at his mistakes.
he = the intelligent person.

    3. Holt regrets his not trying to find a way that works.
he = the dull child

    4. Holt is aware that they have a special outlook on life.
they = intelligent persons (or people)

    5. Holt deplores the fact that it destroys the ability to learn.
it = education

    6. Holt mentions his experimenting.
he = the bright child

III. A. 1. It is mentioned that IQ tests are only indicators of intelligence.

    2. It has been noted that the bright child tries to get in touch with everything.

    3. It is taken into account that we don't start out dull.

    4. It is to be deplored that we lose our ability to learn.

    5. It is to be regretted that the dull child doesn't experiment.

    6. It is hoped that the schools will change.

    7. It is believed that there are actually two different kinds of people.

    8. It is said that we lose our ability to learn.

    9. It is claimed that the bright child wants to find out about life.

    10. It is supposed that "unintelligence" is not just a smaller amount of intelligence.

B. 1. made clear

2. deplored, regretted

3. claimed, supposed

4. regretted, deplored

5. supposed, claimed

C. 1. He makes it clear that a bright child will experiment when he gets into trouble.

2. Some people deplore (regret) the fact that schools destroy the ability to learn.

3. Some people claim (suppose) that bright children have a special outlook on life.

4. Some people regret (deplore) the fact that the dull child doesn't try to find a way that works.

5. People commonly suppose (claim) that schools help children grow intellectually.

IV. A. 1. That education destroys our ability to learn is probable.

2. It is likely that an intelligent person tries to find out all he can about a new situation.

3. It is certain that there is more than one way to skin a cat.

4. Whether the schools will change or not is uncertain.

5. It is improbable that adults will ever learn as much in three years as a child learns in the first three years of life.

6. That an intelligent person has a special outlook on life is likely.

7. It is unlikely that a bright child will try to solve a difficult problem in only one way.

8. That education is supposed to take place in school is certain.

B. Examples: (other sentences are possible)

It is probable that most dull children are not born dull.

It is certain that when a bright child gets into trouble he will experiment.

It is probable that there is a difference between "bright" and "not bright" children.

It is unlikely that "unintelligence" is just a smaller amount of intelligence.

It is improbable that most children are born dull.

It is uncertain whether or not a dull child can break down the wall between him and life in general.

C. Examples: (other sentences are possible)

That most dull children are not born dull is probable.

That a bright child will experiment when he gets into trouble is certain.

That "unintelligence" is just a smaller amount of intelligence is unlikely.

V.   1. OK

2. NO   He mentions that the bright child experiments.
OR: He doesn't mention whether or not. . . .

3. OK

4. NO   Holt thinks that they have a special outlook on life.

5. NO   Some people wonder whether there's. . . .
OR: Some people think that there's. . . .

6. OK

7. NO   It is likely that he has a special outlook on life.

8. OK

9. NO   He doesn't say whether children are born dull or not.

10. OK

VI.   1. probably not

2. no

3. yes

4. probably

5. probably

6. YES

7. YES

8. YES

9. NO

10. NO

Propaganda

Turning Sentences into Objects:
Ing-expressions and Plain Verbs

OVERVIEW

I. Turning sentences into objects by using either *ing* or a plain verb, or by changing the verb into a noun, after the verbs *see, hear, feel, watch*.

II. Comparing completed actions signalled by the plain verb.

III. Using plain verbs after *make* and *let*.

IV. Using *ing*-expressions after *by, in*, and *at*.

V. Summary exercise.

VI. What about meaning?

NOTE: It is recommended that in this lesson you do all three parts—A, B, and C—of the first exercise.

I. Turning sentences into objects by using either *ing* or a plain verb, or by changing the verb into a noun, after the verbs *see hear, feel, watch*.

A. In each pair of sentences below, turn the first sentence into an object in two ways: (a) by changing the verb into an *ing*-form, and (b) by changing the verb into its plain form. Then move the object into the second sentence, putting it where THIS is.

Example:

Do not copy the sentences—just delete, add, and move around, as in the example.

1. The man spoke to the child. We saw THIS.

2. The baby fooled his parents. Did you see THIS?

3. The baby moved in her lap. She felt THIS.

4. The child cried. Did you hear THIS?

B. In the sentences below, sentences have been turned into objects by changing the verb in the sentences into either an *ing*-form or another form. In both cases, whether the *ing*-form or another form is used, the verb has been changed into a noun. Each object is underlined. Your task is to write out the sentence that each object came from, as in the examples.

Examples: She felt the movement of the child.

The child moved.

We saw the shaking of the crib.

The crib shook.

1. He could feel the beating of his heart.

_____

2. She heard the chattering of the children.

_____

3. They saw the departure of the visitors.

_____

4. He watched their observation of the child.

_____

5. We heard his request for a second helping.

_____

6. The baby could hear the smacking of his father's lips.

_____

C. In each pair of sentences below, fill the blank in one sentence with an adjective and the blank in the other sentence with an adverb, choosing related adjectives and adverbs from the lists below, as in the example. The adjective/adverb that you choose for each pair of sentences is your own choice.

Adjectives	Adverbs
careful	carefully
hasty	hastily

intermittent	intermittently
loud	loudly
steady	steadily
sudden	suddenly

Example: (a) She felt the _sudden_ movement of the child.

(b) She felt the child move _suddenly_.

1. (a) He could feel the _____ beating of his heart.
   (b) He could feel his heart beat _____.

2. (a) The baby heard the _____ smacking of his father's lips throughout the meal.
   (b) The baby heard his father's lips smack _____ throughout the meal.

3. (a) She heard the children chatter _____.
   (b) She heard the _____ chattering of the children.

4. (a) They saw the _____ departure of the visitors.
   (b) They saw the visitors _____ depart.

5. (a) We watched them _____ observe the child.
   (b) We watched their _____ observation of the child.

6. (a) We heard his _____ request for a second helping.
   (b) We heard him _____ request a second helping.

II. Comparing completed actions signalled by the plain verb OR *ing* with uncompleted actions signalled by *ing*.

In each of the following sentences there are two forms of the same verb. If the action named by the verb is a completed action, either the *ing*-form or the plain form can be used. If the action named by the verb is not completed, only the *ing* form can be used. In each sentence, underline the form or forms that can be used. The first two sentences are done as examples.

1. We saw the father (taste) (tasting) the baby's food so that the baby would think it was good.

2. We saw him (eat) (eating) the strained carrots, but we left before he had finished them.

3. The little boy saw his sister (eat) (eating) an apple and he took it away from her.

4. He watched him (wheedle) (wheedling) a smile from the child after everyone else had given up.

5. We could feel the baby's crib (shake) (shaking) even when we were in the next room.

6. From the hallway we could hear him (speak) (speaking), but we didn't have time to go in and listen.

7. I heard the child (ask) (asking) his parents for some money to go to the movie.

8. I saw him (leave) (leaving) and so I stopped him and asked him if I could talk with him for a few minutes.

9. He watched the mother (feed) (feeding) her child, but the child refused to eat anything.

10. We heard the children (beg) (begging) their mother to give them some candy.

11. Did you hear the child (refuse) (refusing) to go to bed?

12. You have probably often watched a baby (get) (getting) what it wants.

13. I watched the mother (soothe) (soothing) the child, but she wasn't very successful.

14. Did you hear him (smack) (smacking) his lips when he tasted the carrots?

15. The child screamed when he felt the cat (rub) (rubbing) against his legs.

III. Using plain verbs after *make* and *let*.

Combine each pair of sentences below, as in the example. Do not copy the sentences—just delete and rearrange and be sure the verb form is plain, as in the example.

Example: She let the children ~~DO SOMETHING. They~~ (stayed up until midnight.)

1. Babies know how to make people DO SOMETHING. People will

   pay attention to them.

2. Her father tried to make her DO SOMETHING, but she refused.

   She should eat some strained carrots.

3. They weren't very successful at making the baby DO SOME-

   THING. The baby should eat.

4. The mother let the baby DO SOMETHING for hours because she

   was too tired to carry it around. The baby lay in the crib.

5. They let their children DO SOMETHING last night because the

grandparents were visiting. Their children stayed up until ten.

IV. Using *ing*-expressions after *by, in*, and *at*.
Using the example sentences as models, fill in the blanks in the similar sentences below.

Example sentences:
The cat was chasing the dog mercilessly. We were awakened by THIS.

We were awakened by   (Example 1)   *the cat chasing the dog mer-*
                                       cilessly.
                     (Example 2)   *the merciless chasing of the*
                                       dog by the cat.
                     (Example 3)   *the cat's mercilessly chasing*
                                       the dog.
                     (Example 4)   *the cat's merciless chasing*
                                       of the dog.___

Similar sentences:

1. The man was teaching the child successfully. Our attitude toward him was changed by THIS
Our attitude toward the man was changed by
     (Example 3) his _____
     (Example 4) his _____

2. He uses propaganda techniques cleverly. I'm surprised at THIS.
I'm surprised at
     (Example 1) him (of all people) _____
     (Example 2) _____ use _____
                                  by him (of all people). _____
     (Example 3) his _____
     (Example 4) _____ use _____

3. You explained how to soothe the baby. I was interested in THIS.
I was interested in
     (Example 1) _____
     (Example 2) _____ explanation _____
                                  by you (of all people). _____
     (Example 3) _____
     (Example 4) _____

V. Summary exercise. Put OK in front of the sentences that you consider correct and NO in front of the sentences that you consider

incorrect. Write in corrections for the sentences that you put NO in front of. The first sentence is done as an example.

*No*____ 1. They made him sweeping the floor.

_____ 2. When he saw her eating a candy bar, he took it away from her.

_____ 3. We heard his request loudly for an answer to the question.

_____ 4. We were surprised at his sudden asking of questions.

_____ 5. He watched the plane departing.

_____ 6. They made him clean out the closet.

_____ 7. We heard his loud request for a seat in the front row.

_____ 8. When he saw her eat an orange, he grabbed it out of her hand.

_____ 9. We were startled at his suddenly asking of questions.

_____ 10. They could feel the house shake.

VI. What about meaning?

Place an X in front of the sentence on the right which has a meaning consistent with the meaning of the sentence on the left. The first one is done as an example.

1. They saw him falling off his bicycle and caught him just in time.

  ____ a. They saw him fall
  X   off his bicycle.
  ____ b. They saw him when he was falling off his bicycle.

2. They made her sit down.

  ____ a. She sat down.
  ____ b. She should sit down.

3. They could feel him smiling even though they couldn't see him.

  ____ a. They could feel him smile.
  ____ b. They could feel him when he was smiling.

4. I was surprised at your asking that question.

_____ a. I was surprised at the asking of the question.

_____ b. I was surprised that you were the one to ask the question.

5. He watched him eat his supper.

_____ a. He ate his supper.

_____ b. He was eating his supper but we don't know if he finished it or not.

Answers to Sentence Study—Propaganda

I. A. 1. We saw the man speaking to the child.
We saw the man speak to the child.

2. Did you see the baby fooling his parents?
Did you see the baby fool his parents?

3. She felt the baby moving in her lap.
She felt the baby move in her lap.

4. Did you hear the child crying.
Did you hear the child cry.

B. 1. His heart beat.

2. The children chattered.

3. The visitors departed.

4. They observed the child.

5. He requested a second helping.

6. His father smacked his lips.

C. 1. (a) adjective
(b) adverb

2. (a) adjective
(b) adverb

3. (a) adverb
(b) adjective

4. (a) adjective
(b) adverb

5. (a) adverb
(b) adjective

6. (a) adjective
(b) adverb

II.
1. taste tasting
2. eating
3. eating
4. wheedle wheedling
5. shake shaking
6. speaking
7. ask asking
8. leaving
9. feeding
10. beg begging
11. refuse refusing
12. get getting
13. soothing
14. smack smacking
15. rub rubbing

III.
1. Babies know how to make people pay attention to them.
2. Her father tried to make her eat some strained carrots, but she refused.
3. They weren't very successful at making the baby eat.
4. The mother let the baby lie in the crib for hours because she was too tired to carry it around.
5. They let their children stay up until ten last night because the grandparents were visiting.

IV.
1. his successfully teaching the child
   his successful teaching of the child
2. him (of all people) using propaganda techniques cleverly.
   the clever use of propaganda techniques by him (of all people).
   his cleverly using propaganda techniques
   his clever use of propaganda techniques
3. you explaining how to soothe the baby.
   the explanation of how to soothe the baby by you—of all people.
   your explaining how to soothe the baby.
   your explanation of how to soothe the baby.

V.
1. NO They made him sweep the floor.
2. OK
3. NO We heard his loud request for an answer to the question.
   OR
   We heard his loudly requesting an answer to the question.

4. OK

5. OK

6. OK

7. OK

8. NO When he saw her eating an orange, he grabbed it out of her hand.

9. NO We were startled at his suddenly asking questions. OR We were startled at his sudden asking of questions.

10. OK

VI.   1. b

2. a

3. a

4. b

5. a

Words in Context

Turning Sentences into Subjects and Complements:
(For)To-Expressions with Adjectives and Nouns,
and Variations Thereof

OVERVIEW

I. Turning sentences into complements of adjectives; other ways of saying the same thing. Adjectives: *good (of), stupid (of), thoughtful (of)*, etc.; *good (for), hard (for), difficult (for)*, etc.

II. *It is possible (for-to)* compared with *It is possible (that)* . . .

III. Turning sentences into complements of nouns; other ways of saying the same thing.

IV. Summary exercise.

V. What about meaning?

I. Turning sentences into complements of adjectives; other ways of saying the same thing. Adjectives: *good (of), stupid (of), thoughtful (of)*, etc.; *good (for), hard (for), difficult (for)*, etc.

A. Combine each pair of sentences below, as in the examples. Delete the subject of the first sentence, change the verb to its *to*-form, and move the whole thing to the end of the second sentence. In each sentence underline one of the expressions in parentheses, according to your own choice. When you finish you might want to compare your choices with the choices of your classmates and discuss them.

Examples: (*to tell*
~~He told~~ me the meaning of the word.) It was (<u>nice</u>) (inconsiderate) of him.

(*to tell*
~~He told~~ me the meanings of the words.) It was (<u>easy</u>) (hard) for him.

1. I forgot to bring a dictionary. It was (stupid) (absent-minded) of me.

2. I found the words in the dictionary. It was (easy) (challenging) for me.

3. I guess the meanings of words. Sometimes it is (difficult) (easy) for me.

4. He shared his dictionary with me. It was (thoughtful) (selfish) of him.

5. He will try to guess the meanings of all those words. It will be (interesting) (uninteresting) for him.

6. He knew all the words. It was (clever) (stupid) of him.

7. She guessed the meaning of the word. It was (good) (smart) of her.

8. He figured out a way to use that word. It was (easy) (difficult) for him.

9. He should practice using context clues. It would be (good) (bad) for him.

10. He lent me his dictionary. It was (good) (selfish) of him.

11. Guess the meanings of cognate words. It will sometimes be (easy) (difficult) for you.

12. You hid my dictionary. It was (considerate) (awful) of you.

B. The sentences below are the ones you may have ended up with when you did Part A of this exercises. Your task now is to take each sentence and say the same thing in a different way, as in the examples. Notice that sentences with *of* after the adjective are handled differently from those with *for* after the adjective.

Examples: *He*
          ~~It~~ was nice ~~of him~~ to tell me the meaning of the word.
          (SOMEONE was nice.)

          ~~It~~ was easy for him to tell me (the meanings of the words.) (SOMETHING was easy.) *Or: The words were easy for him to tell me the meanings of.*

1. It was stupid of me not to bring a dictionary.

2. It was easy for me to find the words in the dictionary.

3. Sometimes it is easy for me to guess the meanings of words.

4. It was thoughtful of him to share his dictionary with me.

5. It will be interesting for him to try to guess the meanings of all these words.

6. It was clever of him to know all the words.

7. It was smart of her to guess the meaning of the word.

8. It was difficult for him to figure out a way to use that word.

9. It would be good for him to practice using context clues.

10. It was good of him to lend me his dictionary.

11. It will sometimes be easy for you to guess the meanings of cognate words.

12. It was awful of you to hide my dictionary.

C. The sentences below are ones you might have ended up with when you did Part B of this exercise. The number in parentheses after each sentence indicates the number of the sentence in Part B that it corresponds to.

There are still more ways to say the same thing. Rewrite each of the sentences below in two ways, as in the examples.

Examples: He was nice to tell me the meaning of that word.

For him to tell me the meaning of that word was nice.

Telling me the meaning of that word was nice of him.

The meanings of the words were easy for him to tell me.

For him to tell me the meanings of the words was easy.

Telling me the meanings of the words was easy for him.

1. I was stupid not to bring a dictionary. (1)

_____

_____

2. He was thoughtful to share his dictionary with me. (4)

_____

_____

3. He was clever to know all those words. (6)

_____

4. She was smart to guess the meaning of the word. (7)

_____

5. He was good to lend me his dictionary. (10)

_____

6. You were awful to hide my dictionary. (12)

_____

7. The words in the dictionary were easy for me to find. (2)

_____

8. The meanings of the words are sometimes easy for me to guess. (3)

_____

9. The meanings of all these words will be interesting for him to try to guess. (5)

_____

10. That word was difficult for him to figure out a way to use. (8)

_____

11. Context clues would be good for him to practice using. (9)

_____

12. The meanings of cognate words will sometimes be easy for you to guess. (11)

_____

II. _It is possible (for-to)_ compared with _It is possible (that)_ . . .
Compare these two example sentences. They do not mean the same thing.

(1) It is possible for him to figure out the meaning from context clues.

(2) It is possible that he will figure out the meaning from context clues.

Meaning of (1): He can figure out the meaning from context clues.

Meaning of (2): Maybe he will figure out the meaning from context clues.

Complete the sentences below according to the meaning given for each.

1. It is possible _____

_____

(Meaning: Maybe she doesn't know how to use context clues.)

2. It is usually possible _____

_____

(Meaning: We can usually get the meaning of a word from context without looking it up in the dictionary.)

3. It is possible _____

_____

(Meaning: We can figure out the meaning of "opacity" from the context.)

4. It is possible _____

_____

(Meaning: Maybe he lost his train of thought while he was looking up the word in the dictionary.)

5. It is possible _____

_____

(Meaning: Sometimes you can find a synonym of the new word in the same sentence.)

6. It was impossible _____

_____

(Meaning: He could not bring a dictionary to class today.)

7. It is possible _____

_____

(Meaning: Maybe they got the meanings of most of the words from context.)

8. Sometimes it is impossible _____

_____

(Meaning: Sometimes you cannot use context clues.)

9. It is possible _____

_____

(Meaning: Maybe he didn't select the appropriate dictionary definition.)

10. It is possible _____

_____

(Meaning: Maybe he already knew the meaning of "fission.")

III: Turning sentences into complements of nouns; other ways of saying the same thing.

Study the four example sentences below. All four sentences mean:

He looked up those words. It was a waste of time.

Examples: It was a waste of time for him to look up those words.
Those words were a waste of time for him to look up.
For him to look up those words was a waste of time.
Looking up those words was a waste of time for him.

Using these example sentences as models, fill in the blanks below.
The first one is done for you.

1. It was a waste of time for him to look up those words.
Looking up those words *was a waste of time for him.*

2. It was a hard job for them to follow the train of thought in that article.
For them to follow the train of thought _____
_____

3. It was a pleasant duty for her to read that novel.
That novel _____
_____

4. It was fun for them to learn how to unlock the meanings of unfamiliar words.
Learning how to unlock the meanings of unfamiliar words _____
_____

5. It is too much of a burden for you to carry around a dictionary all the time.
A dictionary is too much of a burden _____
_____

6. It can be a time saver for a reader to use context clues.
Using context clues _____
_____

7. It was a boon for them to learn how to figure out meanings from context.
Learning _____
_____

8. It is a difficult task for a second-language learner to build up a good-sized vocabulary.
For a second-language learner _____
_____

IV. Summary exercise. Put OK in front of the sentences that you consider correct and NO in front of the sentences that you consider incorrect. Write in corrections for the sentences that you put NO in front of. The first sentence is done as an example.

_*No*_   1. It is possible ~~for her~~ that she forgot her dictionary.

_____   2. It was easy for him to analyze the word.

_____   3. It is possible that she forgot her dictionary.

_____ 4. Figuring out the meaning of new words is not always easy for me.

_____ 5. It was nice of you to help me.

_____ 6. It was easy of him to analyze that word.

_____ 7. For you to help me was nice of you.

_____ 8. You was nice to help me.

_____ 9. It is hard for many students to enlarge their vocabulary.

_____ 10. It was nice for him to win the dictionary.

_____ 11. It is usually hard for him to resist looking words up in a dictionary.

_____ 12. To analyze the word it was easy for him.

V. What about meaning?

In each of the following sentences, the underlined adjective refers to either SOMEONE or SOMETHING. Draw a circle around either SOMEONE . . . or SOMETHING. . . . , according to which one the adjective describes. The first two are done as examples.

1. It is good for you to learn how to guess the meaning of words.

   SOMEONE is good. (SOMETHING is good.)

2. It was smart of them to learn several methods of unlocking word meanings.

   (SOMEONE is smart.) SOMETHING is smart.

3. It was good of her to help you with your vocabulary study.

   SONEONE is good.   SOMETHING is good.

4. It was thoughtless of him not to return your dictionary.

   SOMEONE is thoughtless.   SOMETHING is thoughtless.

5. It is hard for me to remember the meanings of some words.

   SOMEONE is hard.   SOMETHING is hard.

6. It will be nice for you to have your own dictionary.

   SOMEONE is nice.   SOMETHING is nice.

7. It was nice of him to help you choose the appropriate definition.

   SOMEONE is nice.   SOMETHING is nice.

8. It is difficult for us to learn words out of context.

   SOMEONE is difficult.   SOMETHING is difficult.

In each item below, put a check in front of the sentence on the right that you think is the closest in meaning to the sentence on the left. The first one is done as an example.

9. I was stupid not to guess that meaning.

   _X_ a. Not to guess that meaning was stupid of me.

   ____ b. Guessing that meaning was stupid of me.

10. Context clues are sometimes impossible to find.

   ____ a. I sometimes find impossible context clues.

   ____ b. It is sometimes impossible for me to find context clues.

11. It is possible for this word to have several meanings.

   ____ a. This word can have several meanings.

   ____ b. Maybe this word has several meanings.

12. It is difficult for him to remember that word.

   ____ a. He is difficult to remember that word.

   ____ b. That word is difficult for him to remember.

13. Looking up those words was a waste of time for him.

   ____ a. For him to look up those words was a waste of time.

   ____ b. For us to look up those words was a waste of time for him.

14. It is possible that he lost his dictionary.

   ____ a. Perhaps he lost his dictionary.

   ____ b. He can lose his dictionary.

Answers to Sentence Study—Words in Context

I. A. 1. It was stupid of me not to bring a dictionary.
   2. It was easy for me to find the words in the dictionary.
   3. Sometimes it is easy for me to guess the meanings of words.
   4. It was thoughtful of him to share his dictionary with me.
   5. It will be interesting for him to try to guess the meanings of all those words.
   6. It was clever of him to know all the words.

7. It was smart of her to guess the meaning of the word.

8. It was difficult for him to figure out a way to use that word.

9. It would be good for him to practice using context clues.

10. It was good of him to lend me his dictionary.

11. It will sometimes be easy for you to guess the meanings of cognate words.

12. It was awful of you to hide my dictionary.

B. 1. I was stupid not to bring a dictionary.

2. The words in the dictionary were easy for me to find.

3. The meanings of the words are sometimes easy for me to guess.

4. He was thoughtful to share his dictionary with me.

5. The meanings of all these words will be interesting for him to try to guess. OR All these words will be interesting for him to try to guess the meanings of.

6. He was clever to know all the words.

7. She was smart to guess the meaning of the word.

8. That word was difficult for him to figure out a way to use. OR A way to use that word was difficult for him to figure out.

9. Context clues would be good for him to practice using.

10. He was good to lend me his dictionary.

11. The meanings of cognate words will sometimes be easy for you to guess. OR Cognate words will sometimes be easy for you to guess the meanings of.

12. You were awful to hide my dictionary.

C. 1. For me not to bring a dictionary was stupid.
Not bringing a dictionary was stupid of me.

2. For him to share his dictionary with me was thoughtful.
Sharing his dictionary with me was thoughtful of him.

3. For him to know all those words was clever.
Knowing all those words was clever of him.

4. For her to guess the meaning of the word was smart.
Guessing the meaning of the word was smart of her.

5. For him to lend me his dictionary was good. (Notice that here there is a meaning change: *good* means *a good thing to do*.)
Lending me his dictionary was good of him.

6. For you to hide my dictionary was awful.
Hiding my dictionary was awful of you.

7. For me to find the words in the dictionary was easy.
Finding the words in the dictionary was easy for me.

8. For me to guess the meanings of words is sometimes easy.
   Guessing the meanings of words is sometimes easy for me.

9. For him to try to guess the meanings of all these words will be interesting.
   Guessing the meanings of all these words will be interesting for him.

10. For him to figure out a way to use that word was difficult.
    Figuring out a way to use that word was difficult for him.

11. For him to practice using context clues would be good.
    (*good = a good thing for him to do*)
    Practicing using context clues would be good for him. OR
    Practicing the use of context clues would be good for him.

12. For you to guess the meanings of cognate words will sometimes be easy.
    Guessing the meanings of cognate words will sometimes be easy for you.

II.   1. It is possible that she doesn't know how to use context clues.

2. It is usually possible for us to get the meaning of a word from context without looking it up in the dictionary.

3. It is possible for us to figure out the meaning of "opacity" from the context.

4. It is possible that he lost his train of thought while he was looking up the word in the dictionary.

5. It is possible sometimes for you to find a synonym of the new word in the same sentence.

6. It was impossible for him to bring a dictionary to class today.

7. It is possible that they got the meanings of most of the words from context.

8. Sometimes it is impossible for you to use context clues.

9. It is possible that he didn't select the appropriate dictionary definition.

10. It is possible that he already knew the meaning of "fission."

III. 1. Looking up those words was a waste of time for him.

2. For them to follow the train of thought in that article was a hard job.

3. That novel was a pleasant duty for her to read.

4. Learning how to unlock the meanings of unfamiliar words was fun for them.

5. A dictionary is too much of a burden for you to carry around all the time.

6. Using context clues can be a time saver for a reader.

7. Learning how to figure out meanings from context was a boon for them.

8. For a second-language learner to build up a good-sized vocabulary is a difficult task.

IV.   1. NO It is possible that she forgot her dictionary.

      2. OK

      3. OK

      4. OK

      5. OK

      6. NO It was easy for him to analyze that word.

      7. NO For you to help me was nice. OR It was nice of you to help me. OR Helping me was nice of you.

      8. NO You were nice to help me.

      9. OK

    10. OK

    11. OK

    12. NO To analyze the word was easy for her.

V.   1. SOMETHING is good.

      2. SOMEONE is smart.

      3. SOMEONE is good.

      4. SOMEONE is thoughtless.

      5. SOMETHING is hard.

      6. SOMETHING is nice.

      7. SOMEONE is nice.

      8. SOMETHING is difficult.

      9. a

    10. b

    11. a

    12. b (NOTE: *a* is an ungrammatical sentence)

    13. a

    14. a

Forms of Address

Turning Sentences into Objects and Complements: That/Ing, That/To, and Split Sentences

OVERVIEW

I. Turning sentences into complements by using *that* and *to* and the sentence paraphrase—after *forget, remember, remind someone (about)*.

II. Turning sentences into complements by using *that* and *to* and the split-sentence paraphrase—after *forget, remember, remind someone (about)*.

III. Using *that*, *ing*, and *to* expressions.

IV. Selecting pronouns before *ing*-expressions.

V. Summary exercise.

VI. What about meaning?

I. Turning sentences into objects by using *that* and *ing* and the split-sentence paraphrase—after *forget, remember, remind someone (about)*.

A. In the following pairs of sentences, change the second sentence into a *that*-expression and insert it into the position filled by SOMETHING.

Example:

Ted forgot ~~SOMETHING.~~ (the fact) that He didn't know her real name. (NOTE: *the fact* is optional)

Or: *about the fact that she had not met him.* that she had not met him

Sue reminded me (about) ~~SOMETHING.~~ She had not met him. (NOTE: When *about* occurs after *remind*, *the fact* must also occur; when *about* does not occur, *the fact* cannot occur.)

Do not copy the sentences. Just add and delete, as in the example.

1. Mrs. Lee reminded me about SOMETHING. She had told me his name twice.

2. Bill forgot SOMETHING. He hadn't told her his name.

3. Did you remember SOMETHING? You had met him before.

4. I remember SOMETHING. She told me her name.

5. Jane remembered SOMETHING. They had met her before.

6. Saroj forgot SOMETHING. The title isn't used with the last name.

7. Kazuko reminded me about SOMETHING. I had introduced them.

8. I forgot SOMETHING. The title goes with the last name.

B. In the sentences below, change the *that*-expression into an *ing*-expression, as in the example. Notice the uses of the pronouns in the example and in the first four sentences.

Example: Ted forgot (about the fact) that he didn't know her real name.

Ted forgot about not knowing her real name.
(he = Ted)

Ted forgot about his not knowing her real name.
(he = either Ted or someone else)

1. Sue reminded me (about the fact) that she had not met him.

_____

(*she* = Sue)

_____

(*she* = either Sue or someone else)

2. Mrs. Lee reminded me (about the fact) that she had told me his name twice.

_____

(*she* = Mrs. Lee)

_____

(She = Mrs. Lee or someone else)

3. Bill forgot (about the fact) that he hadn't told her his name.

___

(*he* = Bill)

___

(*he* = Bill or someone else)

4. Did you remember that you had met him before?

___

(*you* = only you, and so *your* may either occur or not occur, with no change in meaning)

5. I remember that she told me her name.

___

6. Jane remembered that they had met her before.

___

7. Saroj forgot (about the fact) that the title isn't used with the last name.

___

8. Kazuko reminded me (about the fact) that I had introduced them.

___

9. I forgot (about the fact) that the title goes with the last name.

___

C. Write a split-sentence paraphrase for each of the sentences below. Split each sentence by placing *what* in front of the sentence and *was* after the first verb (plus *about*).

Examples:

   what   *was*
   ᶺTom forgot ᶺthat they didn't know each other.

   What   *was*
   ᶺTom forgot ᶺabout their not knowing each other.

Do not copy the sentences. Just add, as in the examples.

1. The man forgot that he didn't know her name.

   The man forgot about not knowing her name.

2. I forgot that I hadn't introduced them.

   I forgot about not having introduced them.

3. Rebecca didn't remember that she had signed her nickname

   to the letter.

Rebecca didn't remember having signed her nickname to the

letter.

4. He forgot that he hadn't signed the guest book.

He forgot about not having signed the guest book.

II. Turning sentences into complements by using *that* and *to* and the split-sentence paraphrase.

   A. In the following pairs of sentences, turn the second sentence into a *that* expression and insert it into the position filled by SOMETHING. Notice that, unlike Part A, *the fact* cannot occur in these sentences.

Example:
        Mr. Webster forgot ~~TO DO SOMETHING.~~ *that* ~~H~~e should have asked her her first name.

Do not copy the sentences. Just delete and add, as in the example.

1. Sumalee reminded me TO DO SOMETHING. I should call her

by her first name.

2. They forgot TO DO SOMETHING. They should have asked

the employees what they call their boss.

3. Mr. Kuykendall never remembers TO DO SOMETHING. He

should call her by her first name.

4. Mrs. Hemenway forgot TO DO SOMETHING. She should have

asked Mrs. Keller what her husband's initials are.

5. Did you remember TO DO SOMETHING? You should sign your

full name.

6. I didn't think TO DO SOMETHING. I should have asked him

what his last name is.

(NOTE: In sentence 6 the meaning changes when the sentences are combined. In the sentence you just wrote, the meaning is: "I *did* ask him what his last name is even though I had an idea that I shouldn't." See the note after sentence 6 in Part B below.)

B. In the sentences below, change the *that* expression into a *to* expression as in the example.

Example: Mr. Webster forgot that he should have asked her her first name.

Mr. Webster forgot to ask her her first name.

1. Sumalee reminded me that I should call her by her first name.

_____

2. They forgot that they should have asked the employees what they call their boss.

_____

3. Mr. Kuykendall never remembers that he should call her by her first name.

_____

4. Mrs. Hemenway forgot that she should have asked Mrs. Keller what her husband's initials are.

_____

5. Did you remember that you should sign your full name?

_____

6. I didn't think that I should have asked him what his last name is.

_____

(NOTE: In sentence 6, when the *that* expression is changed to a *to* expression the meaning of the sentence changes. With the *to* expression, the sentence means: *I didn't think TO DO SOMETHING. I should have asked him what his last name is. Think* means *remember* in this sentence. Compare the note after sentence 6 in Part A above.)

C. Write a split-sentence paraphrase for each of the sentences below. Split each sentence by placing *What* in front of the sentence and *to do + is* OR *was* after the verb, as in the example. The *to* that comes after *is* or *was* is optional.

Example:

Mr. Olsen never remembers to call her by her first name.

1. Naomi didn't think to ask him for his autograph.

2. Mr. Jamieson forgot to sign both copies of the contract.

3. Children usually remember to call adults by their last names.

4. Ken tries to remember to use the proper form of address.

III. Using *that, ing,* and *to* expressions.

Complete each sentence below so that it makes good sense, using the verbs that are given in capital letters. The first one is done as an example.

1. I will sign the book if you remind me *to (sign it).*
_____SIGN

2. The bank won't cash your check if you forget _____
_____ENDORSE

3. After Sarah handed in her paper, she remembered that
_____FORGOT, so
she asked for her paper back and signed her name on it.

4. He forgot that he had met me last year, but I remembered
_____MEET.

5. She says she never criticized him, but I can remember _____
_____SAY.

IV. Selecting pronouns before *ing*-expressions.

In each of the following sentences, draw a circle around each of the items in parentheses which would give the sentence the intended meaning. The symbol for absence of a pronoun is Φ. In some cases two items will be circled and in other cases only one.

Example: Intended meaning: They gathered the data.
I forgot about (Φ, (their,) (them)) gathering the data.

1. Intended meaning: I gave him the data.

I forgot about (Φ, my) giving him the data.

2. Intended meaning: I didn't give him the data.

I forgot about (Φ, my) giving him the data.

3. Intended meaning: I gave him the data.

I didn't think about (Φ, my) giving him the data.

4. Intended meaning: Either the anthropologist or another man collected the data.

The anthropologist mentioned something about (Φ, his, him) collecting the data.

5. Intended meaning: Some man other than the anthropologist collected the data.

   The anthropologist mentioned something about (Φ, his, him) collecting the data.

6. Intended meaning: The anthropologist collected the data.

   The anthropologist mentioned something about (Φ, his, him) collecting the data.

7. Intended meaning: I introduced them.

   My uncle reminded me about (Φ, my) introducing them.

8. Intended meaning: I hadn't introduced them yet.

   My uncle reminded me about (Φ, my) introducing them.

9. Intended meaning: I wrote him a letter.

   I was thinking about (Φ, my) writing him a letter.

10. Intended meaning: I haven't written him a letter yet.

    I was thinking about (Φ, my) writing him a letter.

V. Summary Exercise. Put OK in front of each sentence that you consider correct and NO in front of each sentence that you consider incorrect. Correct the sentences that are not correct. The first one is done as an example.

_*No*_   1. She remembered ~~to have~~ *having* met him before.

_____ 2. He reminded me about my having introduced them.

_____ 3. I didn't think to have asked him what his name is.

_____ 4. What she didn't remember was having introduced them.

_____ 5 She forgot to introduce them.

_____ 6. He forgot about them not knowing each other.

_____ 7. She remembered having met him before.

_____ 8. She forgot to have introduced them.

_____ 9. What she didn't remember was about having introduced them.

_____ 10. I didn't think to ask him what his name is.

_____ 11. He forgot about his having met him before.

_____ 12. What John didn't remember was his having introduced
them to each other last year.

VI. What about meaning?

Read the following sentences and answer the question about each
by putting an X in front of the answer. The first one is done as an
example.

1. John forgot about not knowing the mailman's name.
   Who didn't know the mailman's name?   _____John

   _____someone else

2. She reminded me about having told John my nickname.
   Who had told John my nickname?   _____she

   _____I

3. Bill mentioned something about him having collected some data.
   Who collected some data?   _____Bill

   _____someone else

4. She reminded me to tell them my full name.
   Who should tell them my full name?   _____she

   _____I

5. Sam forgot about them not having been introduced.
   Who had not introduced them?   _____Sam

   _____someone else

6. They forgot about his not knowing her.
   Who didn't know her?   _____they

   _____he

In each item below, put an X in front of the sentence on the right
which you think is the closest in meaning to the sentence on the
left. Number 7 is done as an example.

7. The man forgot that he didn't   _____a. She reminded
   know her last name.   him about his
   not knowing
   her last name.

   _____b. What the man
   knew was that
   he had forgot-

ten her last
name.

8. She didn't remember having signed   _____a. What she didn't
   her nickname to the letter.   remember was
                                                     having signed
                                                     her nickname
                                                     to the letter.

                                              _____b. Her nickname
                                                     was what she
                                                     remembered
                                                     having signed
                                                     to the letter.

9. She reminded me that I had   _____a. She reminded
   introduced them.   me about
                                                     introducing
                                                     them.

                                              _____b. She reminded
                                                     me about my
                                                     having in-
                                                     troduced them.

10. He forgot to go.   _____a. He forgot that
                                                     he went.

                                              _____b. He forgot that
                                                     he should have
                                                     gone.

11. He reminded me to call him   _____a. He reminded
    by his first name.   me about my
                                                     calling him by
                                                     his first name.

                                              _____b. He reminded
                                                     me that I
                                                     should call him
                                                     by his first
                                                     name.

12. She reminded me about having   _____a. She reminded
    told me his name twice.   me that she
                                                     had told me
                                                     his name twice.

                                              _____b. She reminded
                                                     me that some-
                                                     one had told
                                                     me his name
                                                     twice.

Answers to Sentence Study—Forms of Address

I. A. 1. Mrs. Lee reminded me (about the fact) that she had told me his name twice.

   2. Bill forgot (the fact) that he hadn't told her his name.

   3. Did you remember (the fact) that you had met him before?

   4. I remember (the fact) that she told me her name.

   5. Jane remembered (the fact) that they had met her before.

   6. Saroj forgot (the fact) that the title isn't used with the last name.

   7. Kazuko reminded me (about the fact) that I had introduced them.

   8. I forgot (the fact) that the title goes with the last name.

   NOTE: The *that* which introduces the *that* expression can be optionally deleted.

   B. 1. Sue reminded me about not having met him.
      Sue reminded me about her not having met him.

   2. Mrs. Lee reminded me about having told me his name twice.
      Mrs. Lee reminded me about her having told me his name twice.

   3. Bill forgot about not having told her his name.
      Bill forgot about his not having told her his name.

   4. Did you remember (your) having met him before?

   5. I remember her telling me her name.

   6. Jane remembered their having met her before.

   7. Saroj forgot about the title not being used with the last name.

   8. Kazuko reminded me about my having introduced them.

   9. I forgot about the title going with the last name.

   C. 1. What the man forgot (about) was that he didn't know her name.
      What the man forgot about was not knowing her name.

   2. What I forgot (about) was that I hadn't introduced them.
      What I forgot about was not having introduced them.

   3. What Rebecca didn't remember was that she had signed her nickname to the letter.
      What Rebecca didn't remember was having signed her nickname to the letter.

   4. What he forgot (about) was that he hadn't signed the guest book.

What he forgot about was not having signed the guest book.

II. A. 1. Sumalee reminded me that I should call her by her first name.

2. They forgot that they should have asked the employees what they call their boss.

3. Mr. Kuykendall never remembers that he should call her by her first name.

4. Mrs. Hemenway forgot that she should have asked Mrs. Keller what her husband's initials are.

5. Did you remember that you should sign your full name?

6. I didn't think that I should have asked him what his last name is. (Meaning: I shouldn't have asked him what his last name is.)

B. 1. Sumalee reminded me to call her by her first name.

2. They forgot to ask the employees what they call their boss.

3. Mr. Kuykendall never remembers to call her by her first name.

4. Mrs. Hemenway forgot to ask Mrs. Keller what her husband's initials are.

5. Did you remember to sign your full name?

6. I didn't think to ask him what his last name is .(Meaning: I didn't remember to ask him what his last name is.)

C. 1. What Naomi didn't think to do was (to) ask him for his autograph.

2. What Mr. Jamieson forgot to do was (to) sign both copies of the contract.

3. What children usually remember to do is (to) call adults by their last names.

4. What Ken tries to remember to do is (to) use the proper form of address.

III. Sample sentences:

1. I will sign the book if you remind me to (sign it).

2. The bank won't cash your check if you forget to endorse it.

3. After Sarah handed in her paper, she remembered that she had forgotten to sign her name, so she asked for her paper back and signed her name on it.

4. He forgot that he had met me last year, but I remembered that I had met him OR I remembered meeting him OR I remembered having met him.

5. She says she never criticized him, but I can remember that she said he hadn't done a good job OR her saying that he hadn't done a good job.

IV.   1. Φ, my

      2. Φ

      3. my

      4. his

      5. him

      6. Φ, his

      7. my

      8. Φ

      9. my

    10. Φ

V.   1. NO She remembered having met him before.

      2. OK

      3. NO I didn't think to ask him what his name is.

      4. OK

      5. OK

      6. OK

      7. OK

      8. NO She forgot to introduce them.

      9. NO What she didn't remember was having introduced them.

    10. OK

    11. OK

    12. OK

VI.   1. John

      2. she

      3. someone else

      4. I

      5. someone else

      6. he

      7. a

      8. a

      9. b

    10. b

    11. b

    12. a

The Environment and the Automobile

Turning Sentences into Objects and Subjects:
Ing-expressions

OVERVIEW

I. Turning sentences into complements by using *ing* after the verbs *begin, continue, start, resume, finish, stop, keep on, consider*, and *resist*.

II. Two kinds of *ing*-expressions, state and action, in subject position, and the *for-to* paraphrase of the state *ing*.

III. Summary exercise.

IV. What about meaning?

I. Turning sentences into complements by using *ing* after the verbs *begin, continue, start, resume, finish, stop, keep on, consider*, and *resist*.

A. Combine each pair of sentences below, as in the example.

Example: We should consider, ~~DOING SO. (We should ride~~ *riding* bicycles.)

Do not copy the sentences. Just add, delete, and rearrange, as in the example.

1. What will happen if we keep on DOING SO? We use the automobile as our main means of transportation.

2. If we continue DOING SO we will face serious energy problems. We use the automobile as our main source of transportation.

3. We need to begin DOING SO. We should think of changes in passenger transportation.

4. We can't stop DOING SO until we decrease the number of cars. We build highways.

5. Some people will resist DOING SO. They should use mass transit instead of automobiles. ·

6. When a country starts DOING SO, they set a whole chain of consequences in motion. They manufacture automobiles.

7. When a factory finishes DOING SO, the energy requirements for the car are only partially fulfilled. The factory manu-factures a car.

8. We must consider DOING SO even though it will require modifications of many elements in our society. We should make changes in passenger transportation.

9. All children do a lot of walking. People should continue DOING SO all their lives. They should walk.

10. If you haven't walked much since you were a child, you should resume DOING SO. You should walk.

B. Combine each pair of sentences below, filling in the blank with any of the following verbs which you think is appropriate to the meaning of the sentence: *begin, continue, start, resume, finish, stop, keep on, consider,* and *resist.* In cases where more than one verb is appropriate choose only one. The first one is done as an example.

1. He hasn't ridden a bicycle for years, but recently he has

   begun DOING SO. He is (riding one.)

2. Many people wish that the government would _____

   DOING SO. They are building so many highways.

3. If we _____ DOING SO, we may destroy the

   environment. We depend on the automobile for transportation.

4. When you _____ DOING SO, did you resolve to do

   more walking? You listened to the talk about the automobile

   and the environment.

5. How old were you when you _____ DOING SO? You

   drive a car.

6. We must _____ DOING SO. We must look for ways

   to conserve energy.

7. The earth cannot _____ DOING SO forever. It sup-

   plies oil.

8. Did you ever _____ DOING SO? You might buy a

   bicycle.

C. For each of the following sentences do two things: (1) replace
   DOING SO with a verb phrase of your own choice; (2) underline
   the verb in parentheses that you think is appropriate to the sense
   of your sentence. There are no "right" answers in this exercise.
   When you finish your sentences you may want to compare them
   and discuss them with your classmates. The first one is done as
   an example.

   1. Energy problems have caused people to (start, stop, resist)
      DOING SO.

2. A country will (keep on, resist, resume) DOING SO as long as the number of cars increases.

3. If they (stop, finish, start) DOING SO there will be more land for parks.

4. Some people (begin, resist, keep on) DOING SO because they don't want to be personally inconvenienced.

5. It's time to (resist, begin, resume) DOING SO now, even though it will take at least a few decades to abandon the use of cars as the main means of passenger transportation.

NOTE: Three of the verbs in the above sections can be followed by a *to*-expression as well as by an *ing*-expression, usually with the same meaning: *begin, start,* and *continue*. Notice, however, that when *stop* is followed by a *to*-expression, the meaning changes: *stop to talk* means 'stop in order to talk' and *stop talking* means 'cease talking.' The other verbs in the above sections can never be followed by *to*-expressions.

II. Two kinds of *ing*-expressions—state and action—in subject position, and the *for-to* paraphrase of the state *ing*-expression.

A. Change each sentence below into an *ing*-expression in two ways, as in the example.

Example: They build the highways.
State: *(their) building the highways*
Action: *the (or their) building of the highways.*

1. They ride bicycles.
State: _____
Action: _____

2. They carry more passengers.
State: _____
Action: _____

3. They reduced air pollution.
State: _____
Action: _____
(use *reduction*)

4. They discovered an oilfield.
State: _____
Action: _____
(use *discovery*)

5. They maintain highways.
    State: _____
    Action: _____
    　　　　(use *maintenance*)

6. They promoted changes in passenger transportation.
    State: _____
    Action: _____

B. The *action* form of the *ing*-expression can always be used. The *state* form can only be used when the emphasis is on the state of affairs rather than on the action.

　　The sentences below sound somewhat odd to many speakers of English because they use a *state ing*-expression in referring to an action.

　　In each sentence change the *state ing*-expression into an *action ing*-expression. The first one is done as an example.

　　Do not copy the sentences. Just delete and add, as in the first one.

　　The question mark in front of each sentence indicates that it is somehow "odd-sounding."

1. ?~~Their~~ *The* building *of* the highways proceeded rapidly.

2. ?His riding the bicycle was not very skillful.

3. ?Carrying more passengers is not occurring as fast as it should.

4. ?Their discovering an oilfield was not announced to the public.

5. ?Reducing air pollution will happen only when people become more informed.

6. ?Their maintaining the highways was discontinued because of lack of funds.

7. ?Their promoting changes in passenger transportation must start immediately.

C. The *for-to* paraphrase of the *state ing*-expression.
    Only *state ing*-expressions have *for-to* paraphrases.
    Rewrite each of the sentences below in two ways, as in the example.

Example: Their building highways was inevitable.

    a. *For them to build highways was inevitable.*

    b. *It was inevitable for them to build highways.*

1. His riding a bicycle surprised no one.

    a. _____

    b. _____

2. Their (the cars') carrying more passengers is desirable.

    a. _____

    b. _____

3. Their discovering an oilfield was a surprise to everyone.

    a. _____

    b. _____

4. Reducing air pollution requires effort on everyone's part.

    a. _____

    (begin the sentence with *To reduce*)

    b. _____

5. Maintaining the highways was a full-time job.

    a. _____

    (begin the sentence with *To maintain*)

    b. _____

6. Promoting changes in passenger transportation is not easy.

    a. _____

    (begin the sentence with *To promote*)

    b. _____

III. Summary exercise. Put OK in front of the sentences that you consider correct and NO in front of the sentences that you consider incorrect. Write in corrections for the sentences that you put NO in front of. The first sentence is done as an example.

No   1. Shall we resume ~~to discuss~~ *discussing* the problems caused by the automobile?

_____ 2. Some people resist decreasing the use of the automobile.

_____ 3. The building of highways has gone on for years.

_____ 4. Carrying of four passengers in a car would increase the energy-efficiency of cars.

_____ 5. They started talking about the impact of the automobile on the environment.

_____ 6. People should stop using cars as their primary method of transportation.

_____ 7. For them to build the highways proceeded rapidly.

_____ 8. The carrying of four passengers in a car is not common these days.

_____ 9. Some people would not consider to walk if they could ride.

_____ 10. The reduction of air pollution would be welcome.

_____ 11. They should stop to build highways immediately.

_____ 12. The building highways has taken up much land.

IV. What about meaning? For each item below, put an X in front of the sentence on the right which you think is the closest in meaning to the sentence on the left. In two items, both sentences on the right should have X's in front of them. The first one is done as an example.

1. For them to discover an oilfield surprised everyone.

_____ a. They discovered an oilfield to surprise everyone.

___X___ b. It surprised everyone for them to discover an oilfield.

2. People haven't stopped buying cars.

_____ a. People haven't stopped to buy cars.

_____ b. People are still buying cars.

3. To promote changes in passenger transportation is not easy.

_____ a. It is not easy to promote changes in passenger transportation.

_____ b. Promoting changes in passenger transportation is not easy.

4. They began walking to work.

_____ a. They began to walk to work.

_____ b. They began to work to walk.

5. Manufacturing an automobile
takes energy.

_____ a. The manufacture
of an automobile
takes energy.

_____ b. To manufacture
an automobile
takes energy.

Answers to Sentence Study—
The Environment and the Automobile

I. A. 1. What will happen if we keep using the automobile as our main means of transportation?

2. If we continue using the automobile as our main source of transportation we will face serious energy problems.

3. We need to begin thinking of changes in passenger transportation.

4. We can't stop building highways until we decrease the number of cars.

5. Some people will resist using mass transit instead of automobiles.

6. When a country starts manufacturing automobiles they set a whole chain of consequences in motion.

7. When a factory finishes manufacturing a car the energy requirements for the car are only partially fulfilled.

8. We must consider making changes in passenger transportation even though it will require modifications of many elements of our society.

9. All children do a lot of walking. People should continue walking all their lives.

10. If you haven't walked much since you were a child, you should resume walking.

B. 1. He hasn't ridden a bicycle for years, but recently he has begun OR started OR resumed OR considered riding one.

2. Many people wish that the government would stop building so many highways.

3. If we continue OR keep on depending on the automobile for transportation, we may destroy the environment.

4. When you finished listening to the talk about the automobile and the environment, did you resolve to do more walking?

5. How old were you when you began OR started driving a car?

6. We must begin OR continue OR start OR keep on OR consider looking for ways to conserve energy.

7. The earth cannot continue OR keep on supplying oil forever.

8. Did you ever consider OR resist buying a bicycle?

C. The answers are your own choice. You might want to compare what you have written with the answers of some of your classmates.

A few sample answers are given below:

1. Energy problems have caused people to start thinking about the role of the automobile in our environment.
Energy problems have caused people to resist the building of more highways.

2. A country will keep on building highways as long as the number of cars increases.

etc.

II. A. 1. (Their) riding bicycles
The OR Their riding of bicycles

2. (Their) carrying more passengers
The OR Their carrying of more passengers

3. (Their) reducing air pollution
The OR Their reduction of air pollution

4. (Their) discovering an oilfield
The OR Their discovery of an oilfield

5. (Their) maintaining highways
The OR Their maintenance of highways

6. (Their) promoting changes in passenger transportation
The OR Their promotion of changes in passenger transportation

NOTE: The parentheses around *their* indicate that in some sentences it can be deleted.

B. 1. The building of the highways proceeded rapidly.

2. His riding of the bicycle was not very skillful.

3. The carrying of more passengers is not occurring as fast as it should.

4. Their discovery of an oilfield was not announced to the public.

5. The reduction of air pollution will happen only when people become more informed.

6. The maintenance of the highways was discontinued because of lack of funds.

       7. The promotion of changes in passenger transportation must start immediately.

C. 1. a. For him to ride a bicycle surprised no one.
        b. It surprised no one for him to ride a bicycle.

    2. a. For the cars to carry more passengers is desirable.
        b. It is desirable for the cars to carry more passengers.

    3. a. For them to discover an oilfield was a surprise to everyone.
        b. It was a surprise to everyone for them to discover an oilfield.

    4. a. To reduce air pollution requires effort on everyone's part.
        b. It requires effort on everyone's part to reduce pollution.

    5. a. To maintain the highways was a full-time job.
        b. It was a full-time job to maintain the highways.

    6. a. To promote changes in passenger transportation is not easy.
        b. It is not easy to promote changes in passenger transportation.

III.   1. NO Shall we resume discussing the problems caused by the automobile?

     2. OK

     3. OK

     4. NO The carrying of four passengers in a car would increase the energy-efficiency of cars.

     5. OK

     6. OK

     7. NO The building of highways proceeded rapidly.

     8. OK

     9. NO Some people would not consider walking if they could ride.

    10. OK

    11. NO They should stop building highways immediately.

    12. NO The building of highways has taken up much land.

IV.   1. b

     2. b

     3. a, b

     4. a

     5. a, b

Food for Thought

Turning Sentences into Objects and Subjects:
WH Clauses and Split Sentences

OVERVIEW

I. Turning sentences into objects and subjects by using WH words like *who(m), what, which, where, when, how, why.*

II. Reduced WH clauses: *who(m) to see, what to do, when to go,* etc.

III. Turning yes-no questions into objects and subjects by using *whether or not.*

IV. The split sentence paraphrase of WH and *whether or not* clauses.

V. Summary exercise.

VI. What about meaning?

I. Turning sentences into objects and subjects by using WH words like *who(m), what, which, where, when, how, why.*

A. Change the following questions into WH clauses, as in the examples.

Examples: How long have you been interested in food fads?

What do you think about food fads?

no change
What determines food habits?

Do not copy. Just reorder the subjects and verbs and delete as necessary. Remember to delete the question marks.

1. Which meat can we eat?

2. How intelligent can a child be?

3. How long have food fads been with us?

4. How does protein affect the number of brain cells?

5. Where did the use of white rice constitute status?

6. Where did the belief that fish is brain food probably originate?

7. Why do some people eat a lot when they are unhappy?

8. When do some adults drink a lot of milk?

9. What religions forbid the use of pork?

10. Who believed that eating the heart of the lion could increase courage?

B. For each sentence below, do two things: (1) change the sentence into a question beginning with a WH-word; (2) change the sentence into a WH-clause, as in the example.

Example: You think *something* about food fads. (*what*)
Question: *what do you think about food fads* ?
WH clause: Please tell me *what you think about food fads.*

1. *Some* religions forbid the use of pork. (*what* or *which*)
Question: _____
WH clause: Can you tell me _____

2. *Someone* believes that eating a lion's heart increases courage. (*who*)
Question: _____
WH clause: I wonder _____

3. We can eat *some* kind of meat. (*what* or *which*)
Question: _____
WH clause: Did they explain _____

4. A child can be intelligent *to a certain degree*. (*how*)
Question: _____
WH clause: What things influence _____

5. Food fads have been with us *for a certain length of time*. (*how long*)
Question: _____
WH clause: Can you tell me _____

6. Protein affects the number of brain cells *in a certain way*. (*how*)
Question: _____
WH clause: Can you explain _____

7. The use of white rice constituted status *in a certain place.* (*where*)
   Question: _____
   WH clause: Do you know _____

8. The belief that fish is a brain food probably originated *in a certain place.* (*where*)
   Question: _____
   WH clause: Did the text mention _____

9. *For a certain reason* some people eat a lot when they are unhappy. (*why*)
   Question: _____
   WH clause: Tell me _____

10. Some adults tend to drink a lot of milk *at a certain time.* (*when*)
    Question: _____
    WH clause: Do you know _____

C. Complete the sentences below by filling each blank with one of the following WH clauses. The first one is done as an example.

   WH clauses: what white rice meant in many Asian countries
   which meat one can eat
   how intelligent a child can be
   how protein affects the number of brain cells
   what food sometimes provides to the frustrated person.

1. *Which meat one can eat* sometimes depends on one's religion.

2. _____ is emotional satisfaction.

3. _____ may depend on how much protein he gets.

4. _____ was status.

5. _____ was the subject of a research study.

II. Reduced WH clauses: *who(m) to see, what to do, when to go,* etc.

   A. Write the reduced WH clause paraphrase of each of the WH clauses below, as in the example.

   Example: what one should (not) eat *what (not) to eat*

   1. where we should go for a vegetarian meal   _____

   2. when he should order pork   _____

   3. who(m) I should ask about the eating habits of his country   _____

4. how one should grow high
   value foods

   _____

5. how he could increase his
   courage

   _____

6. where he could buy whole
   grain rice

   _____

7. why we should not eat pork _____

B. Fill in each of the blanks in the sentences below with one of the
following reduced WH clauses, as in the example.

how to increase	when to order beef
where to go	who(m) to ask
how to grow	which store to go to.
what to eat	

Example: When there are many restrictions on food, it's hard
(for one) to know *what to eat*_____.

1. Can you tell us _____ for a vegetarian meal?

2. He wanted to know _____ to buy
   whole grain rice.

3. When a person is traveling through many countries it is
   sometimes hard to know _____
   and when to order pork.

4. Can you tell me _____ about the
   eating habits of this country?

5. There is some debate about _____
   high value foods.

6. The primitive hunter thought that he knew _____
   _____ his courage.

C. For each sentence below decide whether or not the WH clause
can be reduced. If it can, write *yes* in the blank in front of the
sentence; if it can't, write *no*. The first one is done as an example.

_*No*_ 1. He asked why they considered fish a brain food.

_____ 2. He wondered why he should not eat pork.

_____ 3. He wanted to know how they grew vegetables.

_____ 4. He wanted to know how he should grow vegetables.

_____ 5. Did you tell them where you would go for a vegetarian meal?

_____ 6. Did you tell them where they should go for a vegetarian meal?

_____ 7. Did you ask them where they would go for a vegetarian meal?

_____ 8. Did you ask them where you should go for a vegetarian meal?

_____ 9. He asked us why he should eat whole grain rice.

_____ 10. He told us why we should eat whole grain rice.

You should have four *yes* answers. Write below the four sentences to which you gave *yes* answers, using the reduced WH clause in each. The first is done as an example.

4. *He wanted to know how to grow vegetables.*

_____

_____

_____

III. Turning yes-no questions into objects and subjects by using *whether or not*.

A. Combine each pair of sentences below in any *one* of the five ways shown in the example.

Example: Did she buy whole grain rice? She didn't say.

(1) She didn't say whether or not she bought whole grain rice.

(2) She didn't say whether she bought whole grain rice or not.

(3) She didn't say whether she bought whole grain rice.

(4) She didn't say if she bought whole grain rice or not.

(5) She didn't say if she bought whole grain rice.

1. Is fish brain food? Do you know?

_____

2. Do Hindus eat pork? She didn't mention this.

_____

3. Should he order beef? He didn't know.

_____

4. Do all religions use food for symbolism? The text doesn't say.

_____

5. Is organic fertilizer the only way to grow high value foods? I wonder.

_____

B. Combine each pair of sentences below, as in the example. Notice that *if* cannot introduce a *whether or not* clause in subject position.

Example: *Whether*   *or not*
,~~Do~~ people away from home drink more milk. ~~THIS~~ is
something for you to investigate.   ^

Do not copy the sentences. Just add and delete as in the example.

1. Do you eat beef or pork? THIS may depend on your religion.

2. Is organic fertilizer necessary to grow high value food? THIS

   seems to be a matter for debate.

3. Could a person eat white rice? THIS depended on his wealth.

4. Has the infant had enough protein? THIS can affect the num-

   ber of his brain cells.

C. For each sentence below decide whether or not the *whether or not* clause can be reduced. If it can, write *yes* in the blank in front of the sentence; if it can't, write *no*. The first one is done as an example.

   Yes 1. He didn't know whether he should eat eggs or not.

   _____ 2. The farmer asked whether or not he should spray the vegetables.

   _____ 3. She didn't tell us whether we should buy white or whole grain rice.

   _____ 4. They didn't say whether we should fast tomorrow or not.

   _____ 5. We asked whether or not she should serve him vegetables only.

   You should have four *yes* answers. Write these four sentences below, using the reduced *whether or not* clause in your sentences. The first one is done as an example.

   1. *He didn't know whether to eat eggs or not.*
   _____
   _____
   _____

IV. The split sentence paraphrase of WH and *whether or not* clauses. Split each of the sentences below by placing *what* in front of it and *was* or *is* after the first verb, as in the example.

Example: *What*   *was*
,She didn't say, whether or not she bought whole grain
^ rice.   ^

1. She didn't mention whether or not Hindus eat pork.

2. He didn't know if he should order beef or not. (Change *if* to *whether*)

3. The text doesn't say whether all religions use food for symbolism.

4. I wonder whether or not organic fertilizer is the only way to grow high value food.

5. I wonder who believes that eating the heart of the lion increases courage.

6. They didn't tell us which day was fast day.

7. He wanted to know how to grow vegetables.

8. They didn't explain to her why white rice is low in nutritional value.

V. Summary exercise. Put OK in fron of each sentence that you consider correct and NO in front of the sentences that you consider incorrect. Write in corrections for the sentences that you put NO in front of. The first sentence is done as an example.

_____ 1. *Whether* If you eat beef or pork may depend on your religion.

_____ 2. They asked him why they should use organic fertilizer.

_____ 3. He wanted to know which meat could we eat.

_____ 4. He told us why he would not eat pork.

_____ 5. Do you know where can find a vegetarian restaurant?

_____ 6. They asked us why to use organic fertilizer.

_____ 7. They asked us which meat they could eat.

_____ 8. Whether or not you eat eggs depends on how strict a
_____ vegetarian you are.

_____ 9. Did he tell you why not to eat pork?

_____ 10. Do you know where we can buy whole grain rice?

VI. In each item below, put a check in front of the sentence on the right that you think is the closest in meaning to the sentence on the left. The first one is done as an example.

1. He explained to us why   _____ a. He explained to us why
   not to use sprays.   he should not use
                                           sprays.
                             ✗ _____ b. He explained to us why
                                           we should not use
                                           sprays.

2. He found out how to get a   ————— a. He found out how he
   high yield from the soil.   got a high yield from
                                             the soil
                              ————— b. He found out how he
                                            could get a high yield
                                            from the soil.

3. They asked us where to   ————— a. They asked us where
   buy beef.   they could buy beef.
                              ————— b. They asked us where
                                            we bought beef.

4. The didn't say whether to   ————— a. They didn't say whether
   serve beef or pork.   we should serve beef
                                            or pork.
                              ————— b. They didn't say whether
                                            they would serve beef
                                            or pork.

5. She told us how to cook   ————— a. She told us how we
   the vegetables.   should cook the
                                            vegetables.
                              ————— b. She told us how she
                                            would cook the
                                            vegetables.

In each item below, fill in the blank in the second sentence with the appropriate noun-clause introducer, using the first sentence as a clue. The first one is done as an example.

6. Strict vegetarians do not eat eggs.
   Can you tell me *which kind of* vegetarians do not eat eggs?

7. Many religions use food for symbolism.
   ————————————— many religions use for symbolism is food.

8. The Hindu religion considers the cow to be a sacred animal.
   Can you tell me ————————— religion considers the cow to be a sacred animal?

9. He doesn't eat pork because it against the rules of his religion.
   Did he explain ————————— he doesn't eat pork?

10. The belief that fish is a brain food originated in some area that has not been identified.
    I can't tell you ————————— the belief that fish is a brain food originated.

Answers to Sentence Study—Food for Thought

I. A. 1. which meat we can eat
       2. how intelligent a child can be

   3. how long food fads have been with us

   4. how protein affects the number of brain cells

   5. where the use of white rice constituted status

   6. where the belief that fish is brain food probably originated

   7. why some people eat a lot when they are unhappy

   8. when some adults drink a lot of milk

   9. that religions forbid the use of pork

  10. who believed that eating the heart of the lion could increase courage

B. 1. What (OR which) religions forbid the use of pork?
Can you tell me what (OR which) religions forbid the use of pork?

   2. Who believes that eating a lion's heart increases courage?
I wonder who believes that eating a lion's heart increases courage.

   3. What (OR which) kind of meat can we eat?
Did they explain what (OR which) kind of meat we could eat?

   4. How intelligent can a child be?
What things influence how intelligent a child can be?

   5. How long have food fads been with us?
Can you tell me how long food fads have been with us?

   6. How does protein affect the number of brain cells?
Can you explain how protein affects the number of brain cells?

   7. Where did the use of white rice constitute status?
Do you know where the use of white rice constituted status?

   8. Where did the belief that fish is a brain food probably originate?
Did the text mention where the belief that fish is a brain food probably originate?

   9. Why do some people eat a lot when they are unhappy?
Tell me why some people eat a lot when they are unhappy.

  10. When do some adults tend to drink a lot of milk?
Do you know when some adults tend to drink a lot of milk?

C. 1. Which meat one can eat

   2. What food sometimes provides to the frustrated person
(Note: In this sentence *what* means 'that which' or 'the thing which')

   3. How intelligent a child can be

   4. What white rice meant in many Asian countries

(Note: In this sentence *what* means 'that which' or 'the thing which')

   5. How protein affects the number of brain cells

II. A. 1. where to go for a vegetarian meal

   2. when to order pork

   3. who(m) to ask about the eating habits of his country

   4. how to grow high value foods

   5. how to increase his courage

   6. where to buy whole grain rice

   7. why not to eat pork

  B. 1. where to go

   2. which store to go to

   3. when to order beef

   4. who(m) to ask

   5. how to grow

   6. how to increase

  C. 1. No

   2. No

   3. No

   4. Yes

   5. No

   6. Yes

   7. No

   8. Yes

   9. No

  10. Yes

    He wanted to know how to grow vegetables.
    Did you tell them where to go for a vegetarian meal?
    Did you ask them where to go for a vegetarian meal?
    He told us why to eat whole grain rice.

III. (Note: Only the *whether or not* version of the "WHETHER OR NOT clause" is given below, but any of the versions illustrated in the example are acceptable.)

  A. 1. Do you know whether or not fish is brain food?

   2. She didn't mention whether or not Hindus eat pork.

   3. He didn't know whether or not he should order beef.

   4. The text doesn't say whether or not all religions use food for symbolism.

   5. I wonder whether or not organic fertilizer is the only way to grow high value food.

B. 1. Whether or not you eat beef or pork may depend on your religion.

2. Whether or not organic fertilizer is necessary to grow high value food seems to be a matter for debate.

3. Whether or not a person could eat white rice depended on his wealth.

4. Whether or not the infant has had enough protein can affect the number of his brain cells.

C. 1. Yes He didn't know whether to eat eggs or not.

2. Yes The farmer asked whether or not to spray the vegetables.

3. Yes She didn't tell us whether to buy white or whole grain rice.

4. Yes They didn't say whether or not to fast tomorrow.

5. No
He didn't know whether to eat eggs or not.
The farmer asked whether or not to spray the vegetables.
She didn't tell us whether to buy white or whole grain rice.
They didn't say whether or not to fast tomorrow.

IV.   1. What she didn't mention was whether or not Hindus eat pork.

2. What he didn't know was whether he should order beef or pork.

3. What the text doesn't say is whether all religions use food for symbolism.

4. What I wonder is whether or not organic fertilizer is the only way to grow high value food.

5. What I wonder is who believes that eating the heart of the lion increases courage.

6. What they didn't tell us was which day was fast day.

7. What he wanted to know was how to grow vegetables.

8. What they didn't explain to her was why white rice is low in nutritional value.

V.   1. NO Whether you eat beef or pork may depend on your religion.

2. OK

3. NO We wanted to know which meat we could eat.

4. OK

5. NO Do you know where we can find a vegetarian restaurant?

6. NO They asked us why they should use organic fertilizer.

7. OK

8. OK

9. OK

10. OK

VI.
1. b
2. b
3. a
4. a
5. a
6. which kind of
7. what (meaning *that which*)
8. which OR what
9. why
10. where

Outline of English Nominalizations

Nominalization is a process whereby a sentence is changed into a clause (by the use of *that* or a WH-word like *who, what, when*, etc.) or into a phrase (by changing the verb into its *ing*-form or *to*-form) and then is used as a subject or an object or a complement in another sentence. Such subjects or objects or complements, which have been made out of sentences, are called *nominals*.

All the Sentence Study lessons in this book give practice in nominalization. The ouline below brings together into one presentation the main points about nominalization which are taken up and practiced in these lessons.

NOTES: The symbol → is to be read "can be changed to."

An asterisk (*) indicates that the sequence following it is not grammatical.

Elements enclosed in parentheses are optional.

References to lessons and their subparts are given as follows: One(I), Two(II), etc.

I. THAT-clauses as subjects

A. A sentence can be changed into a nominal by placing *that* in front of it, e.g.,   One(I)

Almost every language has its share of proverbs. →
that almost every language has its share of proverbs

1. *that* nominals can sometimes be changed into *ing* forms: almost every language('s) having its share of proverbs

2. *that* nominals can sometimes be changed into *for-to* forms: for almost every language to have its share of proverbs

B. These nominals may all be used as subjects of sentences:
One(I)

That almost every language has its share of proverbs doesn't surprise me.

OR

The fact that almost every language has it share of proverbs doesn't surprise me.

189

Almost every language('s) having its share of proverbs doesn't surprise me.

For almost every language to have its share of proverbs doesn't surprise me.

C. Starting sentences with *it*—optional   One(II)

1. A subject *that* nominal can be moved to the end of the sentence with *it* taking its place in front of the verb in the following kinds of sentences:

   a. sentences where the verb is *be* followed by a noun phrase like *a fact, our guess, his idea*, etc., e.g.,

      That people everywhere have much in common is a fact. →

      It is a fact that people everywhere have much in common.

   b. sentences where the verb is a verb like *astonish, surprise*, etc., e.g.,

      That people everywhere have much in common doesn't suprise me.

      It doesn't surprise me that people everywhere have much in common.

   c. sentences in which the verb *be* is followed by an adjective like *probable/improbable, possible/impossible, likely/ unlikely, certain/uncertain*, e.g.,   Four(IV)

      That a person starts off stupid is unlikely. →

      It is unlikely that a person starts off stupid.

   (Note: Sentences starting with *it* are more informal than those starting with *that*.)

2. After *it is possible. . .* , a *for-to* nominal as well as a *that* nominal can occur, but with a difference in meaning, e.g.,

        Six(II)

      It is possible that he will figure out the meaning of the word from context. (This is a guess about the possibility of his figuring something out. Maybe he will figure it out and maybe he won't.)

      It is possible for him to figure out the meaning of the word from context. (This means that he *can* figure out the meaning; that is, he knows how. But no guess is made about the possibility of his actually trying to figure it out.)

D. Starting passive sentences with *it*—optional   Four(III)

1. A *that* nominal which is the subject of a passive verb can also be moved to the end of the sentence with *it* taking its place in front of the verb, e.g.,

(The fact) that IQ tests are only indicators of intelligence is mentioned. →

It is mentioned that IQ tests are only indicators of intelligence.

2. In a sentence which starts with *it, the fact* cannot occur in front of the *that* nominal. However, it is possible to say the following:

The fact is mentioned that IQ tests are only indicators of intelligence.

3. In passive sentences with emotive verbs, like *regret, deplore,* etc. (which express emotional feelings), the verb often takes a *to be* form, e.g.,

(The fact) that we lose our ability to learn is to be deplored. /somewhat formal/

OR

It is to be deplored that we lose our ability to learn. /less formal/

E. Starting passive sentences with *it*—obligatory   Four(III)

1. Whether or not a passive sentence must start with *it* depends on the factivity of the verb.

a. A verb like *mention* is a factive verb. The idea expressed by a nominal which comes after a factive verb is assumed to be true, e.g.,

The truth of *we lose our ability to learn* is assumed in *He mentioned (the fact) that we lose our ability to learn.*

b. A verb like *say* is a non-factive verb. The idea expressed by a nominal which comes after a non-factive verb is not assumed to be true, e.g.,

They say that we lose our ability to learn. →

*That we lose our ability to learn is said. → (obligatory)

It is said that we lose our ability to learn.

II. THAT-clauses as objects

A. A factive verb (see I.E.1.a. above) can take a *that*   One(III)
nominal as its object. Such *that* nominals can be   Four(II)
paraphrased by *ing* nominals, e.g.,   Seven(I)
        Seven(III)

He recalled (the fact) that the Iranians have a similar proverb. →

He recalled the Iranians having a similar proverb.

B. A non-factive verb (see I.E.1.b. above) can take a *that* One(IV)
nominal as its object. However, such *that* nominals cannot be turned into *ing* nominals. Some can be turned into *to* nominals and some cannot.

1. After verbs like *believe* and *suppose*, a *that* nominal can be changed to a *to* nominal, e.g.
   Milner believes that the origin of proverbs lies in the universality of human thought. →
   Milner believes the origin of proverbs to lie in the universality of human thought. /more formal/

2. After verbs of saying like *say, claim, maintain*, the only kind of nominal that can occur is the *that* nominal, e.g.,
   They say that haste makes waste.
   BUT NOT
   *They say haste to make waste.

C. Negating non-factive verbs   Four(VI)

   1. Sentences with non-factive verbs—that is, the verbs of believing, which can take either *that* nominal or *to* nominals—can be negated in two ways, e.g.,

      a. Negating the verb in the nominal
         Milner believes that the origin of proverbs does *not* lie in the universality of human thought.
         OR
         Milner believes the origin of proverbs *not* to lie in the universality of human thought. /formal/

      b. Negating the main verb
         Milner does *not* believe that the origin of proverbs lies in the universality of human thought.
         OR
         Milner does *not* believe the origin of proverbs to lie in the universality of human thought. /formal/

   (NOTE: All the four sentences above convey the same meaning.)

D. Summary of the influence of factive and non-factive verbs on the form of the nominal

   1. Nominals which come after factive verbs like *mention, notice, deplore*, etc,. can be in either the *that* form or the *ing* form.

   2. Nominals which come after non-factive verbs of believing can be in either the *that* form or the *to* form.

   3. Nominals which come after non-factive verbs of saying can be in the *that* form only.

   4. The situation, however, is not so clear cut as statements 1–3 above might suggest. Sometimes the same verb is in one category and sometimes in another, e.g.,

      a. *suppose* can mean 'believe,' and when it does, it can be followed by either a *that* or a *to* nominal, e.g.,

Milner supposes that the origin of proverbs lies in the universality of human thought. →

Milner supposes the origin of proverbs to lie in the universality of human thought. /formal/

    b. *suppose* can mean 'say tentatively,' and when it does, it can be followed by a *that* nominal only, e.g.,

    I suppose that John told you about that.

    BUT NOT

    *I suppose John to have told you that.

E. The split sentence paraphrase of sentences with   Seven(I)
that and *ing* nominals as objects.

    1. Sentences which have *that* nominals or *ing* nominals as objects can have a split sentence paraphrase, e.g.,

    Tom forgot that they didn't know each other. →

    What Tom forgot (about) was that they didn't know each other.

    Tom forgot about their not knowing each other. →

    What Tom forgot about was their not knowing each other.

III. WH-clauses and WHETHER OR NOT clauses as SUBJECTS and OBJECTS

A. Sentences can be turned into WH-clauses by   Nine(I)
replacing appropriate part of the sentence with a related WH word and then moving the WH word to the front, e,g,.

    He lives down by the river. → he lives where → where he lives

    He talked to John. → he talked to who(m) → who(m) he talked to

    He thinks that food fads are interesting. → he thinks what → what he thinks

B. WH-clauses can function as subjects and objects, e.g.,

    Where he lives is a secret.

    I don't know who(m) he talked to.

    Did he tell you what he thinks?

C. WH-clauses can sometimes be reduced to a WH word   Nine(II)
plus a *to* nominal, as in *who(m) to see, what to do, where to go.*
Such reduction can occur when the deleted subject is clear from the rest of the sentence, e.g.,

    He doesn't know where *he* should go. →

    He doesn't know where to go.

    He told *us* what *we* should see. →

    He told us what to see.

(NOTE: In *He asked us where to go*, the full form is *He asked us where he should go*. The deleted subject of *go* is understood to be the same as the subject—not the object—of *ask*.)

D. A yes-no question can be turned into a *whether*   Nine(III)
   or not clause by changing it into statement word order and
   putting *whether or not* in front of it, e.g.,
   Did she buy the rice. →
   she bought the rice →
   whether or not she bought the rice
   as in
   I wonder whether or not she bought the rice.

1. When *whether or not* clauses occur as objects, they can
   have several variations, as follows:
   She didn't say

   whether or not she bought the rice.
   whether she bought the rice or not.
   whether she bought the rice.
   if she bought the rice.
   if she bought the rice or not.

2. When *whether or not* clauses occur as subjects they cannot
   begin with *if*, as in the last two variations above. However,
   they can take the other three variations.

E. Clauses introduced by *whether or not* can be reduced in the
   same way that clauses introduced by WH words can be.

1. Such reduction can occur when the deleted subject is clear
   from the rest of the sentence, e.g.,
   He didn't tell *us* whether *we* should go or not. →
   He didn't tell us whether or not to go.
   He doesn't know whether *he* should go or not. →
   He doesn't know whether or not to go.

2. When the verb is *say* (or a verb is saying, like *indicate* or
   explain) the deleted subject may not be expressed in the
   rest of the sentence—it may just be understood, e.g.,
   He didn't say whether or not to go.
   means
   He didn't say (to *someone*) whether *someone* should go
   or not.

F. Sentences which have WH clauses or *whether or not* clauses
   as objects have a split sentence paraphrase, e.g.,   Nine(IV)
   He wanted to know how to grow vegetables. →
   What he wanted to know was how to grow vegetables.
   She didn't say whether or not she bought whole grain rice. →
   What she didn't say was whether or not she bought whole
   grain rice.

IV. THAT-clause as object compared with WHETHER OR NOT clause
    as object   Four(I)

A. If a *that* clause is used as an object, the meaning is that the idea expressed in the *that* clause is to be understood as true, if the main verb is factive, e.g.,

> Holt doesn't mention (the fact) that it is possible to teach dull children to experiment. (Meaning: It is possible to teach dull children to experiment, but Holt doesn't mention that fact.)

B. If a *whether or not* clause is used as an object, the meaning is that the idea expressed in the *whether or not* clause is open to question, e.g.,

> Holt doesn't mention whether or not it is possible to teach dull children to experiment. (Meaning: is it possible to teach dull children to experiment? Holt doesn't take a stand on this question.)

V. ING nominals as subjects, objects, and objects of prepositions

A. Sentences can be turned into *ing* nominals in two   Five(IV)
ways, e.g.,

1. The cat noisily chased the dog. →
the cat('s) noisily chasing the dog
as in: We were awakened by the cat('s) noisly chasing the dog.

2. The cat noisily chased the dog. →
the noisy chasing of the dog by the cat
as in: We were awakened by the noisy chasing of the dog by the cat.

B. The first kind of nominal (V.A.1. above) is   Eight(II)
sometimes called a state nominal. The second kind (V.A.2. above) is sometimes called an action nominal.

C. State nominals can be derived from either action verbs or state verbs. Action nominals can be derived only from action verbs.

1. State verbs are verbs like *hear, like, seem, know*, which do not normally occur in the progressive form when they are used as main verbs (*is seeming*, *is knowing*, etc.).

2. Action verbs are verbs like *walk, speak, write, listen*, all of which can occur in the progressive form when they are used as main verbs (*is writing, is listening*, etc.).

3. Some nominals derived from action verbs have noun counterparts; for example, *explanation* is a noun counterpart of *explaining*. Noun counterparts behave like action nominals, not state nominals.

D. In object of verb and object of preposition positions, either state or action nominals may occur, e.g.

> I was interested in your explaining how to soothe the baby.

OR

I was interested in your explanation of how to soothe the baby.

E. In subject position, the situation is more complicated.

   1. If the main verb refers to a *process* or *activity*, the action nominal must occur, e.g.,

      The building of the highways proceeded rapidly.

   2. If the main verb refers to a *state of affairs*, then either a state or an action nominal may be used, e.g.,

      Their building of the highways was inevitable.

      OR

      Their building the highways was inevitable.

F. *Ing* nominals which are state nominals can be turned into *for-to* nominals, e.g.,

      Their building the highways was inevitable. →

      For them to build the highways was inevitable.

      OR

      It was inevitable for them to build the highways.

G. Sometimes a pronoun (or noun) occurs in   Seven(IV) front of an *ing* nominal.

   1. When a pronoun occurs, it is sometimes possessive and sometimes objective in form. The rules which determine the choice of form are complicated and have never been adequately described. About all that can be done here is to give some examples to show how the presence or absence of the pronoun and its form (when it is present) can affect meaning.

      I was thinking about calling him by his first name. (*thinking about* means 'considering'—I haven't yet called him by his first name.)

      I was thinking about my calling him by his first name. (*thinking about* means 'remembering'—I have already called him by his first name at some earlier time.)

      He forgot about introducing (OR to introduce) them. (He didn't introduce them.)

      He forgot about his introducing them. (He—or some third person other than he—did in fact introduce them.)

      The anthropologist mentioned something about collecting some data. (Either the anthropologist or the person or persons he spoke to will collect the data.)

      The anthropologist mentioned something about him collecting some data. (Some male other than the anthropologist will collect the data.)

   2. Sometimes the pronoun is obligatorily   Eight(I) deleted when a sentence is changed into an *ing* nominal

and the nominal is placed after certain verbs as an object, e.g.,

> We ride bicycles. →
> our riding bicycles
> as in: We should consider riding bicycles.
> BUT NOT *We should consider our riding bicycles.

H. After some verbs, either an *ing* or a *to* nominal can occur, e.g.,

People should continue walking all their lives.

OR

People should continue to walk all their lives.

They started manufacturing automobiles.

OR

They started to manufacture automobiles.

1. Where either the *ing* or the *to* nominal can be used, there is sometimes a subtle difference in meaning, e.g.,

    a. *He started speaking* means that he in fact spoke.

    b. *He started to speak* doesn't necessarily mean that he in fact spoke. Maybe he started and then stopped before he said a single word.

2. With at least one verb—*stop*—only the *ing* form is a nominal, the *to* form being an adverbial. The meanings are completely different, e.g.,

    a. *He stopped talking* means that he is not talking now, although he was talking at an earlier time.

    b. *He stopped to talk* means that he is talking now, although at an earlier time he was not talking.

3. Notice also the difference between *He forgot*   Three(I) *mailing the letter* (which means that he mailed the letter) and *He forgot to mail the letter* (which means that he did not mail the letter. Notice also *He remembered mailing the letter* (meaning: He recalled mailing the letter) and *He remembered to mail the letter* (meaning: He did not forget to mail the letter—he mailed it.)

I. After a limited number of verbs, like *see, hear, watch,*   Five(I) *observe,* an *ing* nominal can be paraphrased by a plain Five(II) verb, e.g.,

They watched the sun rising. →

They watched the sun rise

J. Sometimes the *ing* nominal after such a verb will cause the sentence to be ambiguous, e.g.,

We saw him eating the fruit. (Does this mean that we saw him eat the fruit or that we saw him while he was eating the fruit? Only context will tell: We saw him eating the fruit, and when he finished he came over to speak to us. As we drove by, we saw him eating the fruit, but we don't know whether he ate all of it or not.)

VI. TO nominals as complements in sentences which cannot be passivized

A. A sentence can be turned into a nominal by deleting   Three(I) the subject and the verb auxiliaries and placing *to* in front of the verb. The resulting nominal can then be used as a complement after certain verbs, e.g.,

I go (OR I would go. →

to go

as in: I prefer to go.

He goes. (OR He should go. →

(for) him to go

as in: I prefer (for) him to go.

B. After some verbs, the *to* nominal can be changed   Three(I) to a *that* clause, e.g.,   Seven(II)

He didn't expect to discomfit the other people with his smiling. →

He didn't expect that he would discomfit the other people with his smiling.

C. It is possible for a main verb to change its meaning, depending on whether it is followed by a *to* nominal or a *that* nominal, e.g.,

I didn't think to ask him his first name. (*think* means 'remember')

I didn't think that I should ask him his first name. (*think* means 'believe')

D. Some sentences with *to* nominals after the verb can   Two(II) have a split sentence paraphrase, e.g.,

I prefer to go. →

What I prefer is to go.

I prefer (for) him to go. →

What I prefer is for him to go.

(Note: When the main verb is *forget, remember* (or *think* meaning 'remember'), or *remind* (and possibly some other main verbs which require that the deleted subject of the nominal always be the same as the main subject, for example, *decide* and *resolve*, the split-sentence paraphrase is likely to include *to do*, e.g., Mr. Olsen never remembers to call her by her first name. → What Mr. Olsen never remembers to do is (to) call her by he first name.)

VII. TO nominals as complements in sentences which can be   Two(I) passivized

A. Sometimes a *to* nominal comes after a main verb plus its object, e.g.,

> The urged him. He should go. →
> They urged him to go. → (passive)
> He was urged to go.

B. Sometimes *from* plus an *ing*-form is used instead   Two(III) of a *to* nominal after certain verbs like *prevent, stop*, and *keep*, e.g.,

> They prevented him. He would come. →
> They prevented him from coming → (passive)
> He was prevented from coming.

(Note: *from* plus an *ing*-form is like a *to* nominal in that it refers to something that has not happened and might not happen. Usually *ing* nominals refer to something that has happened or is happening.)

VIII. Using nominals with predicate adjectives and nouns   Six(I)
    Six(V)

A. Sentences can be turned into complements of adjectives, e.g.,

> It was stupid of me to forget my dictionary.
> It was easy for her to guess the meanings of words.

B. Whether the adjective is followed by *of* or by *for* depends on what the adjective is.

  1. Adjectives like *stupid, clever, smart* describe living things and are followed by of.

  2. Adjectives like *easy, difficult, hard* describe something abstract and are followed by *for*.

  3. Some adjectives, like *good*, can fit into either category, depending on their meaning in particular sentences, e.g.,

> It was good of him to help us.
> It was good for him to mow the lawn.

C. Sentences with *of* and sentences with *for* have different paraphrase possibilities, e.g.,

  1. *of* It was stupid of me to forget my dictionary. →
> I was stupid to forget my dictionary.

  2. *for* It was easy for her to guess the meanings of words →
> The meanings of words were easy for her to guess.
> BUT NOT
> *She was easy to guess the meanings of words.

D. There are some *it* sentences of the *for* kind which have nouns instead of adjectives in their predicates, e.g.,   Six(III)

> It was a waste of time for him to look up those words. →
> Those words were a waste of time for him to look up.

Verb and Adjective Listing

These verbs and adjectives appear in the Sentence Study Lessons. The lesson number and sub-part of the lesson in which the verb or adjective occurs is given in parentheses after each item.

Verbs

advise (Two-I.A.B.)
affect (Nine-III.B.)
allow (Two-I.)
announce (Eight-II.B.)
ask (Two-I.C.)

begin (Eight-I.A.B.C.)
believe (One-IV; Four-I.B.C.)

claim (One-IV; Four-III.A.B.C.)
compel (Two-I.A.B.)
conclude (Four-I.A.)
consider (Eight-I.A.B.C.)
continue (Eight-I.A.B.C.)

decide (Three-II.B.C.)
deny (One-III.B.)
depend on (Nine-II.C.; III.B.)
deplore (Four-II.A.B.; III.A.B.C.)
discontinue (Eight-II.B.)

encourage (Two-I.)
expect (Three-I.; II.A.B.C.)
explain (Nine-I.B.; IV.)

feel (Four-I.A.B.C.; Five-I.A.B.C.; II.)
finish (Eight-I.A.B.C.)
force (Two-I.A.B.C.)
forget (One-III.A.; Three-II.A.C.;
        Seven-I.A.B.C.; II. A.B.C.; III.)

happen (Eight-II.B.)

hear (Five-I.A.B.C.; II.)
help (Two-I.A.B.C.)
hope (Three-I; II.A.B.C.)

imply (One-I.A.B.)
indicate (One-I.A.B.C.)
influence (Nine-I.B.)
intrigue (One-I.A.B.C.; II.)

keep from (Two-III.A.B.C.)
keep on (Eight-I.A.B.C.)
know (Four-I.A.; Nine-I.B.; II.B;
      III.C.; IV.)

let (Five-III.)
like (Two-II.A.B.; Three-I.; II.A.)

maintain (One-IV.; Four-I.A.)
make (Five-III.)
make clear (Four-III.B.; III.C.)
mention (One-III.A.; III.B.; III.C.;
      IV; Four-I.A.B.C.; II.A.B.;
      III.A.; Nine-I.B.; IV.)

note (Four-III.A.)
notice (One-III.A.; Four-I.A.; II.A.B.)

occur (Eight II.B.)
order (Two-I.)

permit (Two-I.A.B.)
persuade (Two-I.)
plan (Three-II.A.B.C.)
prefer (Two-II.A.B.C.; Three-I.; II.A.)
prevent _____ from (Two-III.A.B.C.)
proceed (Eight-II.B.)
promise (Three-II.A.B.C.)

recall (One-III.B.C.; IV.)
regret (Four-II.A.B.; III.A.B.C.)
remember (Three-II.A.C.; Seven-I.A.B.C.;
      II.A.B.C.; III.)
remind (Seven-I.A.B.; II.A.B.)
require (Eight-II.C.)
resist (Eight-I.A.C.)
resolve (Three-II.A.B.C.)
resume (Eight-I.A.C.)

say (One-IV; Four-I.A.; III.A.;
      Nine-III.A.C.; IV.)

see (Five-I.A.B.; II.)
seem (Nine-III.B.)
start (Eight-I.A.B.C.; II.B.)
stop (Eight-I.B.C.)
stop _____ from (Two-III.A.B.C.)
strike (One-I.A.)
suggest (One-I.C.)
suppose (One-IV.; Four-III.A.B.C.)
surprise (One-I.A.B.; Eight-II.C.)

take into account (Four-III.A.)
tell (Nine-I.A.; II.B.; III.C.; IV.)
think (Four-I.A.B.C.; Seven-II.A.B.)

urge (Two-I.A.B.)

want (Two-II.A.B.C.; Three-I; II.A.)
watch (Five-I.A.B.C.; II.)
wish (Two-II.A.B.; Three-I.; II.A.C.)
wonder (Four-I.A.B.; Nine-I.B.; II.B.; IV.)

Adjectives

absent-minded (Six-I.A.)
aware (One-III.B.; Four-II.B.)
awful (Six-I.A.B.C.)

certain/uncertain (Four-IV.A.B.C.)
challenging (Six-I.A.)
clever (Six-I.A.B.C.)
considerate (Six-I.A.)

desirable (Eight-II.C.)
difficult (Six-I.A.B.C.)

easy (Six-I.A.B.C.; Eight-II.C.)

good (Six-I.A.B.C.)

hard (Six-I.A.)

inevitable (Eight-II.C.)
interesting (Six-I.A.B.C.)

likely/unlikely (One-II.; Four-IV.A.B.C.)

nice (Six-I.A.C.)

possible/impossible (One-II.; Six-II.)
probable/improbable (Four-IV.A.B.C.)

selfish (Six-I.A.)
skillful (Eight-II.B.)
smart (Six-I.A.B.C.)
stupid (Six-I.A.B.C.)

thoughtful (Six-I.A.B.C.)